THE
ENTREPRENEUR'S
GUIDE TO MAKING
YOUR FIRST
MILLION

THE
ENTREPRENEUR'S
GUIDE TO MAKING
YOUR FIRST
MILLION

How to go from $0 to $1M in 12-18 Months

WILLIAM U. PEÑA, MBA

Dedication

To Matthew and Max, my sons, who give me
the best reason to work less and set the right
priorities in my life.

To my wife, Genie, who has put up with me for the
last two decades and is willing to continue.

To my friends at the 100X Entrepreneur's Club,
you gave me a vision that anything is possible
if you truly believe.

And to God, who has been, and will
always be, my friend.

CONTENTS

100X ENTREPRENEUR'S CLUB

Check out the 100X Entrepreneur's Club
If you want to be part of a community of like-minded individuals who are on their way to $1M in 12-18 months, then join our list of over 277,000 students.

Join the 100X Entrepreneur's Club for FREE today:
100xClub.ai

$0 to $1M Workbook
If you want the 130+ page PDF companion workbook for this Masterclass, you can purchase a copy here:
https://www.100xbusinessadvisor.com/workbook.

PREFACE

It was March 2009. The housing crisis had just crushed the economy. I was doing a few calculations to see how badly it had impacted my finances.

And when I finished, I couldn't believe my eyes.

I was 4 million dollars in debt.

To say I felt terror was an understatement. I thought I was going to get arrested or my kids were going to be sold into slavery like they had done years ago.

I sat there for a while, trying not to break down crying, when the obvious next question popped into my head.

"So what are you going to do now?"

Well, the one thing I needed was time to figure it out. That's because the creditors hounded me daily through aggressive phone calls and letters.

I thought about filing for bankruptcy. But bankruptcy was the atomic bomb of solutions, so I wanted to save it till the last resort. Instead, I researched loopholes that could give me the time I needed to figure things out.

It just so happened that because the government intervened in the housing crisis, it temporarily froze all attempts to force students to pay their debts.

So, I decided to return to school and get my master's degree.

I borrowed even more money to meet my financial needs, which gave me time to decide what to do. More importantly, it gave me the time to honestly understand how entrepreneurship really worked.

You see, after that experience, I swore this kind of business failure would never happen to me again. I was determined to learn all the most successful principles of entrepreneurship, or I was going to die trying.

And you know what?

I did.

Though it was challenging, I learned and applied every success principle I could find from that day on.

Fast-forward to 2024, and since then, I have built two 8-figure businesses, working only a few hours a week. I've been able to retire myself and my parents, and I have boosted my net worth by millions of dollars.

And my favorite: I settled my 4-million-dollar debt for pennies on the dollar, so now I am totally debt-free.

How did I do it?

Using the entrepreneurial success principles I learned.

And these principles are all going to be found in this book.

My promise to you is that if you follow these universal entrepreneurship success principles, you will make $1M in the next 12-18 months.

No B.S., no fluff. Just proven systems that will put you in the best winning position to change your tax bracket.

So, if you are ready to embark on this journey, I ask that you commit to one thing.

Taking action.

Like a key in an ignition determines whether the car will run or not—so taking action will determine whether you will succeed or not.

Therefore, as long as you're committed to that, the sky is the limit to how much money you can make. And, if you need motivation, just ask yourself this question:

"What kind of impact will making $1M in the next 12-18 months have on me, my family, and my future?"

Meditate on that for a minute.

Then strap yourself in because you are about to go on the ride of your life.

Will Peña, MBA
Weston Florida
April 2024

YOUR ROADMAP TO $1M IN 12-18 MONTHS

Welcome to the $0 to $1M in 12-18 Months Masterclass. My name is Will Pena, and over the next few pages, I'll teach you everything you need to know to take your business from zero to one million dollars in revenue in just 12 to 18 months.

This is not just a pipe dream or an empty promise. I'm about to share with you the exact strategies, principles, and systems I've used to build not one but two 8-figure businesses in record time. And now, I want to help you do the same.

Why am I qualified to teach this? Well, let me give you a quick rundown of my entrepreneurial journey.

I've been self-employed for over 20 years, but I kept hitting a ceiling in my businesses for a long time. I had some success, but it seemed to come crashing down eventually. In fact, in 2009, as I mentioned previously, I ended the year with $4 million in debt.

I returned to school, got my MBA, and started working as a business consultant. But even though I had those three letters next to my name, I still didn't know what I was doing. I was good at regurgitating what I read, and my clients paid me for it.

But then, in 2014, everything changed. I lost all my clients and found myself with just $6 in my bank account and rent due. I asked my wife for help, but with eyes full of belief in me, she said, "You'll figure it out." So, I decided to take a leap of faith and do something I had been putting off: I hosted a passive income workshop.

I invited everyone I knew, hoping three or four people would attend. I also charged $2000 for a passive income training program, figuring that if just one person bought it, I could pay my rent and have a little left over to start a business.

Well, not only did 20 people show up at that workshop, but I ended up selling not one but four programs. Overnight, my bank account went from $6 to over $8006. From that moment on, I was hooked on entrepreneurship.

After that, I started an import/export business selling binoculars to birdwatchers. Within 18 months, that business had generated over $1 million in revenue. A few months later, I made my first $1 million in a month. A few years later, it made over $20 million.

Then, I started a children's Book publishing company. That business hit the million-dollar mark in just 12 months and went on to do over $25 million in the span of a few years. It's still going strong today.

After these adventures, I decided to take a break, and I retired for eight years. But recently, I decided to come out of retirement and do it again.

I set myself a challenge: to go from zero to $1 million in 12 months or less. But this time, I thought, why do it alone? Why not find a group of ambitious, hungry, growth-minded entrepreneurs and do it together?

And that's how this Book was born.

The Time is Now

You see, in the time since I was "retired," the opportunities for entrepreneurs have exploded. What took me years to achieve is now possible in a matter of months, thanks to the power of the internet, social media, AI, and the global economy. There are even 15-year-olds out in the world making millions of dollars in just a few short months.

In fact, there are now over 62 million millionaires worldwide, with 24 million in the US alone. If a 7-year-old toy reviewer (Ryan Kaji) can build a $20 million business, then what's stopping you from making your first million?

I truly believe that if I could do it, if all these other millionaires could do it, then you can, too. The key is to have the right roadmap, the right vehicle, and the right support system.

And that's exactly what this Book will provide you. Over the following 13 chapters, I'm going to give you:

1. **The Roadmap**: The step-by-step knowledge and strategies you need to succeed as an entrepreneur and make your first million.
2. **The Vehicle**: The proven business models and systems to take you from zero to $1M.
3. **The Guide**: That's me, someone who's been there, done that, and can help you navigate the journey.
4. **The Group**: A community of like-minded entrepreneurs to support, encourage, and hold you accountable.

With these four elements in place, your chances of hitting that $1M mark increase exponentially.

It's like trying to get through the Amazon jungle. It seems insurmountable at first, but with a map, a trail, a guide, and a group, it becomes not only doable but enjoyable.

It's Time to Change Your Thinking

Now, I want to address a few common doubts and fears that might be holding you back:

- Maybe you're starting from scratch and don't believe it's possible because you've never done it before.
- Maybe you have an established business, but you hit a ceiling every time you try to grow.
- Maybe you offer a service but don't know how to scale without selling your time.

These are all valid concerns. But here's the truth: none of these things matter as much as you think.

Because, in this book, I'm going to teach you the principles of how to think like an effective entrepreneur. I call it 100 Thinking.

100X Thinking comes from the idea that you can get 10X the results with 10X less time, effort, resources, and money. 10 times 10 equals 100—hence, 100X.

I will show you how to build a $1M business, working just 2-4 hours a day and eventually 2-4 hours per week. How? By focusing on leverage, the 20% activities that generate 80% of results, and by constantly asking how to do more with less.

This is how I generated $1M in revenue in my binoculars business, working just a few hours a week. It's also how I scaled my publishing company to $25M while spending more time with my family than in my business.

And it's how you're going to make your first million and do it faster than you ever thought possible.

Now, I want to be clear: I can't guarantee you'll hit $1M in 12 months. But as the saying goes, if you shoot for the stars, you might just hit the moon. Even if you "only" get to $500K or $800K in revenue, that's still a life-changing amount of money. And more importantly, you'll have the skills and the mindset to get to $1M and beyond.

The other reason I chose the 12–18-month timeframe is that it creates urgency. It forces you to move fast, make decisions, and take massive action. With the tools and strategies I'm going to teach you, you can compress timeframes and achieve in a year what might normally take a decade.

What You Can Expect

So here's what you can expect from this Book:

We'll cover the timeless principles of entrepreneurship and the latest tactics and strategies for the modern digital economy. I'll share case studies and examples from my own businesses and from other successful entrepreneurs.

But this isn't just about theory—it's about application. After each chapter, you'll have specific action steps and exercises to implement what you're learning immediately.

And, if you want the support and accountability of a community to keep you on track, join our newsletter at **100xclub.ai**.

The way I've structured this Book is like building a skyscraper:

1. Your mindset is the foundation—nothing else matters without the right mental models and beliefs.
2. The principles of entrepreneurship are the steel frame—they support everything else.
3. The specific strategies and tactics are the individual floors and rooms where the real work happens.

4. Constant improvement and optimization are the interior design—this is how you make your business a place people want to be.
5. And your community is the people who bring the building to life—because business is ultimately about relationships.

If you commit to showing up, doing the work, and supporting your fellow entrepreneurs, then I do not doubt you will achieve extraordinary results.

Here's my challenge to you: for the next few weeks, make this Book your #1 priority. Block off the time in your calendar. Show up every day. Read every page. Do every exercise. Take every action. Participate fully.

If you do that and give it your all, then a year from now, your business and your life will look very different. You'll have a business that generates more revenue in a month than most people make in a year. You'll have the freedom, the impact, and the wealth you deserve. You'll be part of the $1M Entrepreneur's Club.

It won't be easy. There will be challenges, setbacks, and moments of doubt. But you're not in this alone. You have me, and thousands of other entrepreneurs reading this book who are on the same journey. We're going to do this together.

So take a deep breath. Get excited. Because your journey to $1M starts now.

Let's do this!

If you want more proven systems to help you make your first million faster, join the 100X Entrepreneur's Club for FREE today: **100xClub.ai**.

Chapter 1

THE MILLION DOLLAR MINDSET SHIFT

I don't know if you can relate, but when I first thought about starting my own business, I felt sick to my stomach.

I thought it would be the hardest thing in the world, especially when all the businesspeople I knew worked seven days a week and looked ten years older than they were.

In fact, the idea that starting a business would be extremely hard kept me from doing so for at least a decade. What was funny was that I was a business consultant at the time, teaching other people how to build their businesses. But I swore I'd never start my own business because my clients looked miserable.

Luckily for me, I had the privilege of meeting a group of businesspeople who were not only making millions but also working only

5-10 hours a month. They were happy and healthy, had a lot of time for their family, and enjoyed their lives.

To say my mind was blown was an understatement. I didn't even know this existed or was even possible.

Surprisingly, after talking to these happy millionaires, the biggest difference I found between these people and all the other miserable businesspeople I worked with was one thing.

Mindset.

The Million-Dollar Mindset Shift

I want you to picture this: You're standing at the base of a towering mountain, staring at the peak representing your dream of entrepreneurial success.

But you're carrying a backpack loaded with self-doubt, limiting beliefs, and fear of failure. With each step, the pack seems to grow heavier, slowing your climb and making every obstacle feel insurmountable.

Now imagine setting down that heavy pack and discovering it was never necessary. Imagine feeling a surge of energy and clarity as you realize that the only thing holding you back is the weight of your own thoughts.

Suddenly, the path ahead looks brighter, the climb feels invigorating, and you know deep down that you have what it takes to reach the summit.

This is the power of the million-dollar mindset shift.

If you're like most aspiring entrepreneurs, you have a burning desire to turn your passion into profits. You want to break free from the 9-5 grind, escape the self-employment trap, make a meaningful impact, and create extraordinary wealth and freedom.

But a nagging voice in your head whispers, "Who am I to do this? What if I fail? Do I really have what it takes?"

Here's the liberating truth: Your success as an entrepreneur is determined not by your circumstances, skills, or connections but by your mindset. The beliefs you hold, the stories you tell yourself, and the habits you cultivate will either propel you toward your goals or keep you stuck in mediocrity.

In this chapter, we'll explore the psychological secrets of entrepreneurs who have achieved great success. You'll discover how to rewire your brain for abundance, resilience, and relentless growth.

Whether you're just starting your entrepreneurial journey or have been in the game for years, the million-dollar mindset is your key to unlocking the success you desire.

So set down the backpack of limiting beliefs, lace up your boots, and get ready to think like an unstoppable entrepreneur. Your climb to the million-dollar summit starts now.

Mastering Your Mindset—The Key to Entrepreneurial Success

"Ugh, I have all these doubts and negative thoughts in my head, like someone else is doing my idea better, I don't have the talent, or it seems so far-fetched to make a million dollars..."

Sound familiar? If you're an aspiring entrepreneur, you've likely struggled with this kind of self-doubt and mental friction that keeps you from accomplishing your ambitious goals.

Here's the hard truth: Entrepreneurship is 20% luck, 30% skills and strategy, and a whopping 50% mindset and character. If your mindset is not aligned with your goals, your chances of success are slim. It will feel like climbing a steep mountain with a 100-pound pack weighing you down.

But when you develop the mindset and character of an effective entrepreneur, everything changes. It's like going from painfully trudging uphill to effortlessly skiing downhill, with gravity doing most of the work.

Suddenly it's no longer a matter of if you'll reach your goal of making your first million, but when.

In this book, we'll help you make that critical mindset shift—from being plagued by limiting beliefs to embodying the attitudes and habits of successful entrepreneurs.

We'll teach you how to reframe self-doubt, visualize your success, immerse yourself in motivation, and take consistent action to make your entrepreneurial dreams a reality.

So, let's begin.

The 7 Mindsets of Successful Entrepreneurs

It all starts with the 7 Mindsets of Entrepreneurial Success.

Successful entrepreneurs share a set of core mindsets that enable them to navigate challenges and achieve extraordinary results. Adopt these ways of thinking, and you'll set yourself up to win:

1. Abundance Mindset
The Abundance Mindset comes from believing that you have endless opportunities and possibilities. Not only are opportunities abundantly available, but you also believe they are easily accessible to anyone willing to take action.

This is by far the most significant difference between the wealthy and rich, and the poor and middle class.

2. Focus on the Gain
Focusing on the Gain means focusing on your progress, not your distance from your goal. Instead, you celebrate the progress you make each day, no matter how small. Practically, this is as simple as thinking of three areas in your life where you made progress each day.

3. Be Flexible
Flexibility is the choice to adapt to your changing circumstances. It is understanding and embracing the fact that unexpected situations will not only happen, but you welcome them. You welcome them

because you understand their value in opening new opportunities for you.

4. Embrace Uncertainty

Embracing Uncertainty is a mindset where, instead of chasing certainty, you accept the reality of life's uncertainty. So, instead of running away from unwelcome, unpleasant, unexpected, and unwanted circumstances, you embrace them. You use these circumstances to help you grow stronger, become better, and give you access to new opportunities you wouldn't have experienced otherwise.

5. Practice Non-Attachment

Non-attachment is the practice of not attaching yourself too strongly to an outcome, idea, person, opportunity, goal, or anything else. Especially in the business environment, where 99% of your ideas don't work, it's best not to attach yourself to any one idea too strongly. Instead, learn how to hold things lightly so that when you must, you can let them go quickly and pivot rapidly to something better.

6. Focus Only on What You Can Control

The ability to focus only on what's within your control will gradually expand your influence. Therefore, being clear about what you can control and focusing on pulling those levers will help you have the biggest influence in any circumstance.

7. Think 100X

100X Thinking is a mindset focused on finding solutions that will 10X your impact while using 10X less time, effort, resources, and money. Like the two wings of an airplane, it is the balance between pursuing massive results while using massive leverage to get those results. In other words, going after large-scale and exponential returns in a very short period of time.

With these mindsets, not only will you be equipped to succeed—but you'll also have a lot more fun along the way. Challenges will energize you rather than drain you. You'll get into a state of flow where your work feels effortless and rewarding.

For example, when I was at one of the lowest financial points in my life, where I couldn't even pay rent, I felt like giving up. But instead of giving in to my discouragement, I chose abundance, embraced the situation, and pivoted. I also decided to try something I had never tried before.

That brave choice led me to make more money in a day than I had made in the previous three months. Later, it was the jumpstart I needed to make my first million in less than 18 months.

How about you? After looking at this list, which of the seven mindsets do you most need to cultivate?

Here is an exercise to help you grow in these mindsets.

Reflection Exercise

1. What is one of the biggest doubts that you have right now about going from $0 to $1M in 12-18 Months?

2. Ask these 4 Truth questions about that doubt:
   - Is that doubt really true?
   - Why not? (give 3-5 reasons)
   - What is true?
   - Why is that true? (give 3-5 reasons)

3. What are you going to believe from now on?

From personal experience, I can confidently tell you that with the right mindset and character, you'll gain all the clarity and momentum you need to go from zero to $1 million and beyond.

The 10 Commitments of Unstoppable Entrepreneurs

But mindset alone isn't enough. You also need to develop your character. Mindset is the inner game of entrepreneurship; character is the outer game.

The simplest way to define character is the sum total of the habits you build and the commitments you make. Therefore, choosing the right habits and commitments will create the foundation for your entrepreneurial success.

Here are the ten greatest character commitments of successful entrepreneurs. Commit to practicing these ten key practices, and it will guarantee that you will reach your million-dollar goal sooner than you can imagine.

1. Choose Meaningful Goals

Select goals that deeply inspire you. Don't just choose a goal to escape some pain or try to prove something to someone.

The more meaningful the goal, the more of your destiny you control.

2. Commit to Massive Action

Adopt an action-orientation mindset and commit to learning by doing. 80% of your growth will come from taking action, not just acquiring knowledge.

3. Embrace Creativity & Resourcefulness

View obstacles as opportunities to innovate. If one path is blocked, get creative and find another way.

4. Cultivate Tenacity

Bring pig-headed determination to your ventures. You may pause or pivot but decide that you'll never quit.

5. Commit to Continuous Learning

Treat every challenge as a chance to learn and grow. See your journey as a constant evolution.

6. Work on Mindset & Mastery Together

Like two wings of an airplane, devote time to growing your inner and outer game. Master your craft while continually elevating your thinking.

7. Imitate, Then Innovate

Begin by modeling what's already working. Test the proven process first before trying to reinvent the wheel.

8. Make Growth Non-negotiable

Regularly assess how you can improve your mindset, processes, skills, and strategies. Invest in your growth.

9. Focus on the Vital Few

Zero in on the 20% of activities that drive 80% of your results. Ruthlessly cut the rest.

10. Be Decisive

Make the best decisions you can with the information you have. Commit and course correct as you go. And, if in doubt, make a decision.

These commitments form the foundation of the character of a successful entrepreneur. Without them, you may have a great mindset but lack the grit and discipline to reach your full potential.

I experienced the power of these commitments when I started learning about passive income. Even though, at that point, I had the mindset and the training, I just kept hitting a ceiling in how much money I was making.

Then, I committed to sticking to these ten commitments and set a goal of being financially free in three years. To my surprise, I became financially free seven months later because these principles kept me laser-sharp and helped me reach my goal at an explosive speed.

The 4-Step Process to Entrepreneurial Transformation

If you're fired up to embed these mindsets and commitments, you may be wondering where to start. Use this 4-step process to begin your entrepreneurial transformation:

1. Transformation

Notice your limiting beliefs or doubts, and eliminate them by asking the 4 Truth questions from the previous exercise:

1. Is that really true?
2. Why not? (give 3-5 reasons)
3. What is true?
4. Why is that true? (give 3-5 reasons)

2. Visualization

Spend 5 minutes a day vividly imagining your million-dollar goal achieved. Visualize the evidence of your success and feel the positive emotions of that success now.

This practice helped me go from 6 to 7 figures and then to 8 figures.

3. Saturation

Consume motivational content from entrepreneurs who have achieved what you want. Watch videos, read books, attend events, and upgrade your peer group.

I read 100-200 books a year and watch YouTube videos every night to saturate myself and speed up my growth.

4. Implementation

Take consistent action to test your ideas and make steady progress. Focus on the vital few activities that create massive results.

Think "Now, Not How," and take action as soon as possible.

By dedicating yourself to this 4-step process, you'll begin to hardwire the mindsets of successful entrepreneurs. Whenever you notice yourself slipping into doubt or inaction, return to this process to get back on track.

Conclusion: Your Million Dollar Mindset Awaits

We've covered a lot of ground in this chapter, from the critical importance of mindset and character to successful entrepreneurs' specific attitudes and habits. By now, you understand that making your first million starts from the inside out.

You have a choice. You can let your doubts and fears hold you back from your potential. Or you can commit to transforming yourself into an unstoppable entrepreneur. You can stay stuck in scarcity and limitation. Or you can adopt an abundance mindset and see endless opportunities. You can shrink from challenges and stay in your comfort zone. Or you can embrace uncertainty and view obstacles as chances to grow.

The path won't always be easy. You will be tested and stretched outside your comfort zone. But if you commit to the mindsets and commitments we've covered, you will have the psychological foundation to overcome any challenge.

Start by getting clear on your most meaningful goals. Not just the numbers in your bank account but the deeper reasons why you're driven to succeed.

Then, commit to the 4-step Transformation, Visualization, Saturation, and Implementation process. Condition yourself for success by reframing limiting beliefs, imagining your goals achieved, surrounding yourself with inspiration, and taking consistent action.

As you begin to embody the mindsets and character of an unstoppable entrepreneur, you'll be amazed at how your external reality begins to shift. You'll attract new opportunities and resources. You'll face challenges with newfound courage and resilience. And you'll gain unstoppable momentum on your journey from zero to $1 million and beyond.

Your million-dollar mindset is waiting to be unleashed. Decide today that you're willing to do the inner and outer work of an unstoppable entrepreneur. Commit to transforming your psychology and upgrading your habits. Stay grounded in your purpose and keep your vision front and center.

ACTION STEPS

1. **Watch 10-20 YouTube Videos about how to go from $0 to $1M.**

   • This will help convince your mind that it is possible when you see other people doing it as well.

   • Starter Story on YouTube is an excellent source of case studies of entrepreneurs that have gone from $0 to $1M in 12-18 months.

If you want more proven systems to help you make your first million faster, join the 100X Entrepreneur's Club for FREE today: **100xClub.ai**.

Chapter 2

18 PRINCIPLES FOR ENTREPRENEURIAL DOMINATION

For as long as I can remember, I've felt like I was always falling behind and trying to catch up.

In school, I felt like I was always behind everyone else. In sports, I was the last one picked. Even when it came to hobbies, I felt like I was the clueless one who couldn't seem to get it.

The biggest reason was that I didn't know how the rules worked. In school, I didn't pay much attention (probably because of ADHD), so I fell behind a lot. And because I didn't know the rules, everything after seemed really confusing.

Sports were similar. I grew up in a rough neighborhood, so my mom never let me go outside. So when I finally played basketball or baseball in the play yard, I was the oddball who kept missing plays. Again, I didn't know the rules.

I found myself in a similar situation when it came to entrepreneurship. I invested a lot of money and effort, but after a few years, I had very little to show for it.

But I finally decided that enough was enough. I was sick and tired of always falling behind, so this time, I decided that I would do whatever it took to understand the rules of entrepreneurship.

Through this process, I came to one of the most powerful realizations of my entire life. And that is:

"As long as you know the rules, beating the game is easy."

After that, it was easy to make money in entrepreneurship. In fact, it became so easy that I couldn't help but make money.

Now, I want to teach you the rules of entrepreneurship that I learned so that it will be easy for you to beat the game as well.

The 18 Commandments of Entrepreneurial Success

Imagine you're sitting down to play a high-stakes game of poker. The chips are stacked high, the competition is fierce, and the pressure is on. But there's just one problem: you don't know the rules. Without a clear understanding of the game, your chances of walking away a winner are slim to none.

The same is true in business. If you want to succeed as an entrepreneur, you need to know the rules of the game. You need a set of guiding principles that will keep you on track, help you make smart decisions, and ultimately lead you to victory.

By following these principles, you'll be able to navigate the chaotic world of entrepreneurship with confidence and clarity.

So, let's dig in.

The Customer is King

1. The customer always comes first.
Your main responsibility is to ensure your customer is satisfied with your product or service. Without customers, you have no business.

Therefore, the most important principle is that the customer must be the center of your business.

As the earth revolves around the sun, your business must revolve around the customer.

2. Partner with your customers.
You are forming a long-term relationship with your customers, like a marriage. If you want a great relationship with your customers, you will need to constantly communicate with them, meet their needs daily, and keep improving your offerings over time.

If you neglect this, your customers will quickly leave you for someone else. But if you prioritize this, your customers will reward you with great business success for years to come.

3. Find customers you love.

Now that you understand the commitment your customers require, it only makes sense to find customers you love. Because it's tough to serve people you don't like.

Therefore, serving customers becomes easy when you genuinely care about them. So make sure you choose customers who not only value what you offer but also with whom you want to build a lasting relationship.

4. Demand determines dollars.

If you're working too hard to market and sell your product, there's a good chance you have the wrong product. This is because an irresistible product will practically sell itself.

In other words, you need to find out what your customers desperately want first; then, you build your product, service, and business around that.

Take Action

5. Operate your business on two levels.

Businesses usually grow on two levels: incremental and exponential. Both are important, so you need to devote the right amount of time, effort, and resources to each.

Focus a small amount of your time on the areas of the business that bring incremental growth. But devote the lion's share of your time and effort to exponential growth opportunities and explosive, game-changing possibilities.

6. Embrace "Now, not how."

"Now, not how," is one of my favorite phrases made famous by Noah Kagan in his book Million Dollar Weekend. This phrase calls you to take action immediately on your ideas.

In other words, instead of getting stuck trying to figure things out now so you can take action later—instead, learn to take action now and figure things out later.

Even a small action is better than no action at all.

7. Just ask.

Everything you want or need is just an ask away. Leverage your network, and don't be afraid to make requests, whether it's for a sale, a favor, or an opportunity.

The truth is that you are one ask away from your next big opportunity.

8. Put out many offers.

Alex Hormozi once told a story that goes like this: If you knew every time you rolled a double six on a pair of dice, you would get $10k, how often would you roll the dice?

He was saying that success in business is a numbers game. Keep making offers and putting yourself out there. Statistically, if you make enough offers, you will eventually land a sale or find a winning solution.

Play Smart

9. Learn the rules before you play the game.

In any business venture, you need to take action and begin testing the waters as soon as possible. But once your idea is validated, don't dive in headfirst without a good strategy.

Study best practices and learn from the successes of others. Because you can only win the game if you know the rules. So, learn the rules well so you can use them, bend them, and even break them.

10. Focus on the vital few.

The 80/20 rule states that 80% of your results will come from 20% of your efforts. Therefore, you need to learn how to identify and relentlessly focus on the 20% of activities that drive the biggest returns.

By doing this, every choice you make will bring outsized returns while using the least amount of your time and effort.

11. EADS everything else.

Then what do you do with the 80% of the tasks you don't do?

For tasks that don't directly drive revenue, Eliminate, Automate, Delegate, or Simplify (EADS). This way, the necessary tasks still get done, but you keep your time and your business lean and efficient.

12. Work only with the best.

Mediocrity is the enemy of greatness. Or, as some would say, the greatest enemy of the great is the good.

Instead of helping your business grow, hiring good or mediocre people will actually cause your business to stall.

Therefore, you need to surround yourself with only top talent and not settle for mediocrity. This will not only exponentially grow your business but also make the experience a whole lot more enjoyable.

Money Matters

13. Don't spend money until you make money.

There is a teaching that says you need to spend money to make money. What people need to understand is that this teaching only applies if you are already making money.

When you're starting a business and don't know if the market wants what you are offering, you need to spend the least amount of money possible. Only spend money after you know people want what you have to offer.

So, in the beginning, bootstrap wherever possible to avoid unnecessary expenses. Get creative and learn how to make money without spending money. Then, when the money comes, you will have trained yourself to make a lot of money without spending much.

14. Follow the money.

As you try out different business ideas, you'll be tempted to focus your attention evenly, therefore dividing your attention.

Instead, learn to focus most of your energy on your biggest money-maker. In other words, follow the money.

For example, give 80% of your time to the biggest money-making ideas and give new ideas and ventures 20% of your attention. Once these new ventures make you even more money, you can switch most of your attention to the new money maker.

Mindset is Everything

15. Success is inevitable.

As I mentioned previously, entrepreneurship is not a question of if you will succeed, but when. Persistence is the key.

Therefore, having a resilient mindset and absolutely believing that you will be successful will keep you going even when you may not see immediate progress.

Ultimately, if you don't give up, you will be successful.

16. You are the cause of every outcome.

Taking extreme ownership of all the outcomes in your business empowers you to use your greatest resource: your ability to change.

Therefore, take full responsibility for your business results. If you don't like the outcomes you're getting, change your actions.

17. Create routines and guardrails.

The greatest obstacle to business success is the founder's character. Our character weaknesses are the weak link in our ability to execute and do what is necessary to build our business. Even our discipline can be unreliable.

The good news is that a good routine can overcome a weak character. Therefore, rely on routines, systems, and safeguards to keep you on track and keep you doing what needs to be done.

18. Think 100X.

Lastly, the world is full of opportunities to grow your business exponentially. This means you are not doomed only to build a business that generates incremental results.

Therefore, we need to constantly look for ways to get 10X bigger results with 10X less time and effort. What I call 100X.

By doing so, you will strap rockets to your business and take it to heights that neither you nor the world would believe are possible.

By internalizing these principles and making them an integral part of your entrepreneurial operating system, you'll be well on your way to making your first million.

These principles aren't just theory. By applying just a few of these principles, I built an 8-figure business working a few hours a week.

In all honesty, I didn't enjoy building that business much. Now, on the other hand, I am putting all these principles into practice, especially the third principle of finding customers I love. I am on track to build a new business from $0 to $1M in 12-18 months, but this time, I'm loving every minute of it.

But don't just take my word for it. Put these principles into practice and see for yourself how they can transform your business and your life.

Reflection Exercise

1. Take one of the principles that resonates with you in this list.

2. Try practicing that principle for 30 days.

3. At the end of the 30 days, ask yourself: Did this principle improve my business or make it worse?

4. If it made it better, keep doing it!

The path to $1M is paved with smart decisions, strategic focus, and relentless execution. By following these guidelines, you'll be able to cut through the noise, zero in on what really matters, and achieve your entrepreneurial goals.

Conclusion: Your Million-Dollar Destiny Awaits

You now hold the ultimate blueprint for entrepreneurial success, the sacred principles that have guided countless business heroes to the promised land of 7-figure success.

But your journey is far from over. It's only just begun.

The 18 Commandments are not a magic wand you can wave to conjure up a million-dollar business instantly. They are a set of tools, a framework, a way of being that you must embody and apply every single day. They are the foundation upon which you will build your empire, brick by painstaking brick.

As you go forth and put these principles into action, remember that success is not a destination, but a journey. There will be obstacles and setbacks, trials and tribulations, moments of doubt and despair.

But with the 18 principles as your guiding light, you'll have the resilience to weather any storm, the adaptability to pivot when necessary, and the relentless forward momentum to keep pushing towards your goals.

Most importantly, you'll discover that the true reward of entrepreneurship is not just financial freedom and material success, but the person you become in the process. By living and breathing these 18 principles, you'll unleash your full potential as a leader, a visionary, and a force for good in the world.

So, get ready to inspire others with your example and leave a legacy that endures long after you're gone.

ACTION STEPS

1. Action Item 1:

- Just Ask: Practice asking by asking five business establishments this week for a 10% discount.

2. Action Item 2:

- Watch another 10-20 videos on how to make $1M.

If you want more proven systems to help you make your first million faster, join the 100X Entrepreneur's Club for FREE today: **100xClub.ai**.

Chapter 3

CHOOSING YOUR ENTREPRENEURIAL BUSINESS MODEL PART 1

I have a secret to share with you.

When I returned to entrepreneurship, I thought I wouldn't have a clue how to maneuver through this new economy.

But after doing the research, what was truly mind-blowing to me was how much easier it is to make money now than it was years ago. There are 10X more opportunities to make millions, and it's also 10X easier to do it.

In today's economy, even 15-year-old kids make more money in a month than their parents have made in 10 years of working.

What stood out most to me was how many types of businesses can make you $1M, and how easy they are to start.

Therefore, I researched the top 10 business models that consistently bring $1M paydays, and in this chapter, I want to share what I learned with you.

Choose Your Vehicle

Imagine standing in the world's most incredible car lot, with an awe-inspiring selection of gleaming, high-performance vehicles spread out before you. Each is a marvel of engineering, a sleek and powerful machine built for speed, efficiency, and unrivaled success.

But here's the catch—you can only choose one.

And this isn't just any ordinary choice. The car you select will be your partner, companion, and workhorse on your journey. It will carry you through the twists and turns, ups and downs, and the exhilarating freeways of your new adventure.

So, how do you choose? Do you go for the sleek and sexy sports car, with its breakneck speed and head-turning style? Or do you opt for the reliable and sturdy SUV, with its unwavering stability and impressive hauling capacity? You may be drawn to the eco-friendly electric model's cutting-edge technology and low operating costs.

The truth is there's no one "right" choice. What matters most is finding the car that fits you like a glove and that aligns with your strengths, goals, and style.

And that's precisely what choosing a business model is all about.

Think of this chapter as your personal showroom, where you'll get an up-close and personal look at the top 10 business models for achieving $1M in record time. Each model is a different make and model of entrepreneurial vehicle, with its own set of features, benefits, and potential drawbacks.

We'll pop the hood on each one, showing you what makes it tick and how it performs in real-world conditions.

You'll discover the blazing acceleration of E-commerce, the unmatched fuel efficiency of SaaS, and the rugged dependability of Service Businesses. You'll marvel at the sleek lines of Affiliate Marketing, the spacious interior of Information Products, and the cutting-edge technology of Mobile Apps.

But we won't just leave you kicking the tires. By the end, you'll have all the information you need to make an informed decision and choose the business model that's right for you.

You'll know the pros, the cons, and the potential pitfalls of each option, and you'll have a crystal-clear vision of how to use your chosen vehicle to blaze a trail to 7-figure success.

So buckle up, adjust your mirrors, and get ready to put the pedal to the metal. Your million-dollar ride awaits, and the open road of entrepreneurship is calling your name.

The Top 10 Proven Business Models for Hitting $1M in 12-18 Months

"Which business model should I choose? There are so many options, and I don't want to pick the wrong one!" If this sounds like the anxious voice inside your head, you're not alone. Aspiring entrepreneurs often find themselves paralyzed by the sheer number of potential paths to $1M, each with its own allure and challenges.

But here's the good news: just like many different cars can get you from Point A to Point B, there are multiple business models that can transport you to the land of 7-figure success. The key is finding the model that aligns with your strengths, interests, and resources—the entrepreneurial vehicle that feels custom-built just for you.

In these next two chapters, we'll be taking an in-depth look at the top 10 business models that have consistently produced $1M earners in 12-18 months or less. We'll break down the pros and cons for each model, examining factors like profit margins, startup costs, scalability, and competition. By the end, you'll have the knowledge and confidence to choose the business model that will put you on the fast track to $1M.

So buckle up, put on your entrepreneur hat, and let's dive into the high-octane world of million-dollar business models.

In this chapter, we will start with business models that cost the least and are easiest to start. In the next chapter, we will look at more complex models that bring a huge return.

1. Service Businesses

I wanted to begin with service businesses because this is the business model many entrepreneurs choose when they start their journey.

A service business is the simplest of all business models. It is simply when you provide a service for someone for a fee. That can range from marketing services to graphics to window washing or accounting. The number of service businesses is endless.

Here are the pros and cons you can expect from a service business:

⊘ **Pros:**
- Sky-high profit margins (over 80%).
- Zero startup costs.
- Simple to start.

⊗ **Cons:**
- Low potential value at sale (unless productized).
- High competition.
- Difficult to scale.

🔓 **Key to Get to $1M:**
Most service businesses never reach the $1M mark because they naturally depend on one person: you. Since your time and effort are limited, your business will be limited.

Therefore, the key to reaching $1M from a service business lies in changing the format you use to deliver your service. For example, productizing many of your services (converting your service into a product) makes it easier to scale your business to $1M. Also, automating and systemizing your business to run without you will make it easier to scale and rapidly grow.

Last, selling high-ticket products and services is another way to achieve $1M in revenue quicker because you will sell less while making more.

2. Affiliate Marketing

Affiliate Marketing is when you sell other people's products and services for a commission. You could sell online on a dedicated landing page you create that gets a lot of online traffic. Or you can also sell on a social media platform (like TikTok) where you already have a large audience, and sponsors will pay you to sell their products to your audience.

Affiliate marketing is another popular and proven way to make $1M quickly in today's market, especially since today influencers engage with audiences in the millions.

⊘ **Pros:**
- Solid profit margins (20-60%).
- Low/no startup costs.
- Easy to start.
- Highly scalable.

⊗ **Cons:**
- Low/no potential value at sale.
- Cutthroat competition.

Key to Get to $1M:

The biggest challenge with affiliate marketing is competition for eyeballs. Therefore, spending the time to build a large audience or partnering with influencers with large audiences will help accelerate the path to $1M.

Having excellent skills with online ads (Google or Facebook) can also give you an edge in accelerating your growth. Last, using new, trending platforms like TikTok can also give you an edge, especially because its growth is on an exponential upward trend.

3. eBooks and Print Books

Writing eBooks and print books is another business model with a strong history of people having earned $1M in 12-18 months.

It is the oldest of all the business models, but it is still as effective today as ever. People will always want to read a good book, whether fiction or nonfiction. And if your book catches their interest, it can also capture the interest of millions of other readers globally.

The low startup cost and easy scalability also make it a great business model for new entrepreneurs to try out.

✓ **Pros:**
- Free or low-cost to create.
- Simple to get started.
- High potential value at sale.
- Easily scalable through online distributors.

Ⓧ **Cons:**
- Low profit margins (but it has high-volume potential).
- Competitive market.

🔒 **Key to Get to $1M:**

The key to making $1M is to identify demands and trends before you write your book. Preselling your books will give you a good idea of where the market demand is. If no one buys your pre-sales, then don't write the book. If hundreds are buying your presales, then it is the validation you need to write your book.

Looking at trends through bestseller lists is also a way to identify what readers are in demand for. Also, the principle of putting out many offers applies here as well. The more books you put out, the better the chance you will write the next global bestseller.

4. Print-on-Demand

Print-on-demand is when you sell products like T-shirts, mugs, prints, etc., that don't have inventory but are created "on demand" after they are sold. Usually, you're only required to provide the design, and then a manufacturer will print your product as it is sold.

The low cost of entry and simplicity make it another great business model for new entrepreneurs.

The actual product you are selling is your creativity or the creativity of your design team. Then, partnering with a manufacturer and a large marketplace like Etsy or Amazon will give you everything you need for a built-in market for your products.

⊘ Pros:
- Free or low startup costs.
- Simple to start.
- No inventory to manage.

⊗ Cons:
- Low profit margins.
- High competition.
- Low potential value at sale.

🔓 Key to Get to $1M:

Like other commerce-based businesses, the key to growth will be identifying high-demand products. Therefore, best-seller lists are a significant source of inspiration for identifying trending, high-demand products you can imitate and improve on.

Due to its ease of scalability, another key to scaling a print-on-demand business is creating more designs. Once you've identified a market that is in demand and you have successfully sold some products, you can easily create more designs for the marketplace.

5. Information Products

Information products provide educational material to teach or train individuals on a topic. These include written or video training, online courses, newsletters, and eBooks. Masterminds, group or individual coaching programs, or communities are other means of selling information to those seeking it.

The benefit of information products is that you can make money selling them and receive sponsorships from brands interested in reaching your audience.

Information products also provide the unique opportunity to sell high-ticket coaching programs to customers interested in higher-value services as well.

⊘ **Pros:**
- Very high profit margins (70-90%).
- Low/no startup costs.
- Simple to start.
- Medium to high potential value at sale.
- Easily scalable.

⊗ **Cons:**
- Highly competitive.

🔓 **Key to Get to $1M:**
Information products thrive under the idea that the bigger the better. The bigger the audience you build, the more opportunities you have to sell your information products to many more people. Also, the bigger the reputation you build by putting out quality content, the bigger your audience will get and the more you can sell.

Another benefit of selling information products is its high-ticket pricing potential. If you can convince your audience of your value, you can charge very high prices for your services. If you can deliver the outcome, you can price your expertise according to whatever your buyer is willing to pay, which can be in the tens of thousands and even millions of dollars.

Conclusion: Full Steam Ahead!

We've explored five incredible business models that have proven to generate millions in record time, even for new entrepreneurs. From the simplicity and low startup costs of Service Businesses and Print-on-Demand to the scalability and high-profit margins of Affiliate Marketing, Ebooks, and Information Products, each model offers a unique path to 7-figure success.

In the next chapter, we'll explore even more powerful business models that, while more complex, offer the potential for exponential returns. So stay tuned, stay focused, and, most importantly, take action. Your million-dollar business is waiting for you to claim it.

Let's keep this entrepreneurial train moving forward, full steam ahead!

ACTION STEPS

1. Pick the business model from this list that you will pursue for the next 90 Days.

2. Watch 10-20 YouTube Videos on that business model until you feel like you understand how the rules work for that model.

If you want more proven systems to help you make your first million faster, join the 100X Entrepreneur's Club for FREE today: **100xClub.ai**.

Chapter 4

CHOOSING YOUR ENTREPRENEURIAL BUSINESS MODEL PART 2

Making my first million dollars was a lot easier than I thought it would be. I think the biggest reason is that I just copied what I saw other people doing on YouTube and did it myself.

Success leaves clues, so I was determined to learn everything I could from successful business owners. Once I found the business model that fit me best at the time (e-commerce), I researched every successful entrepreneur in the space. I copied everything I saw, followed every instruction, made some improvements along the way, and didn't quit until I succeeded.

And just like they made a million dollars, I made a million dollars.

In the same way, the business models that you've already read about, and the following business models we will discuss—have made more millionaires in less than 18 months than any other business models out in the market today.

Therefore, as you read through all these business models, choose the one that fits you best. Then, devote yourself to learning everything you can about that business model, and your success will be guaranteed.

The Top 10 Proven Business Models Continued

6. E-commerce—White Labeling

E-commerce white labeling is the practice of buying products from one company, rebranding them, and selling them as your own.

White labeling is by far one of the quickest ways to get to $1M in revenue in a very short period. This is because once you find a product in high demand, you can ramp up your sales very quickly by having it sold by a big retailer site like Amazon or by buying a lot of ad traffic to your online store.

⊘ **Pros:**
- Rapid growth potential (especially during holidays and special events).
- Decent potential value at sale.
- Easy to scale by adding more products.

⊗ **Cons:**
- High startup and growth costs.

- Medium effort/complexity (managing inventory, logistics, customer service).
- Intense competition.

 Key to Get to $1M:

The most important key to getting an e-commerce white label business to $1M is to keep testing until you find products in high demand. The key is to check bestseller lists to identify the most successful generic products, then recreate and improve them with your brand. Then, you continue to release new products until you get to $1M in revenue. The best part is that holidays and special event days help you reach your goal even quicker.

7. E-commerce—Dropshipping

Dropshipping is when you buy a branded product wholesale, add a premium, and sell it retail. The money you make comes from the difference between the wholesale price and the retail premium you add. Dropshipping is unique because the supplier manages all the inventory, ships to the customer for you, and takes care of all customer inquiries and returns.

Dropshipping is another business model that has made many individuals $1M in a very short period, mainly because of its low cost of entry and easy scaling ability.

⊘ **Pros:**
- Rapid growth potential.
- Low/no startup costs.

- Simple to set up and run.
- Easy to scale and automate.

Ⓧ **Cons:**
- Razor-thin profit margins (10-20%).
- Very low business sale value.
- Highly competitive.

🔓 **Key to Get to $1M:**

Like white labeling, finding products in high demand is the key to getting to $1M faster. Then, continue adding more products until you make your first $1M.

Having a large established social media audience or establishing partnerships with influencers with large audiences will also accelerate your sales and get you to $1M more quickly.

Last, selling your product lines on new, trending platforms (like TikTok Shops) is also an easy way to 10X your results.

8. SaaS (Software as a Service)

Saas, or software as a service, are software apps and programs you develop and sell that provide a recurring service for customers. The obvious benefit of SaaS products is that you only create them once, but you can sell them over and over again.

Besides the high margins and easy scalability, the ultimate benefit of SaaS products is the sky-high price potential a SaaS business can reach at sale. Ten times annual recurring revenue (ARR) is not uncommon.

For example, if you get your SaaS business to $100K ARR, you can easily find a buyer who will pay you $1M or more for the business.

Pros:
- Massive profit margins (80-90%).
- Effortless scalability.
- Sky-high potential value at sale (10X+ annual recurring revenue).
- Attractive to investors.

Cons:
- Steep startup costs (although lower with no-code options).
- High effort/complexity to develop and maintain.
- Brutal competition (often from well-funded startups).

Key to Get to $1M:
The main accelerator that can catapult a SaaS business to $1M is generating significant interest in your product while you develop it. This could come from selling the product while creating it, taking deposits, or building a large waiting list of people who want to be the first to try it.

Once you're ready to launch, you can leverage your built audience to gain quick sales and have them become your brand advisors and affiliates, spreading the word to more people.

Ultimately, the real difference maker will be the product quality because the greater the people's experience with it, the more they will spread the word about it.

9. Mobile Apps

Like SAAS products, mobile apps are applications created for mobile phones. People love convenience, so having apps on your phone makes a huge convenience for customers and, therefore, creates a high demand.

The one significant difference between SAAS and mobile apps is that mobile apps are sold on an online store, like the App Store (Apple) or Google Play (Google). This can be both a blessing and a curse because you can get great exposure to millions of buyers looking for apps (blessing). Still, the sponsors of these stores charge considerable fees to be listed in their stores (curse).

⊘ **Pros:**
- Huge potential reach through app stores.
- High scalability.
- Attractive to investors.
- High potential value at sale.

⊗ **Cons:**
- Very Intense competition.
- High development costs and complexity.
- High App store fees and high cancelation (churn) rates.

🔓 **Key to Get to $1M:**
Like SAAS products, the main accelerator for mobile apps to reach $1M is generating significant interest in the product through creating a waiting list. Once you're ready to launch, you can leverage your built audience, which becomes your

brand advisors and affiliates that can spread the word to more people as well.

Ultimately, just like with SAAS products, the real difference maker will be the quality of the product. The better the mobile app, the more viral it will become.

10. Agencies

An agency is when a service provider expands by hiring multiple providers to serve even more people. Software designers, AI automation agencies, graphic designers, etc., would fall into this category.

Though scaling is difficult, if you can continue to adequately serve a growing number of new customers and effectively manage an expanding team, you will be able to scale as large as you'd like, easily breaking the $1M revenue mark.

⊘ **Pros:**
- High profit margins (50-60%).
- Low startup costs (leverage your expertise).

⊗ **Cons:**
- More complex to manage (dealing with employees/contractors).
- Challenging to scale.
- High competition.
- Low potential value at sale (unless productized or systematized).

Key to Get to $1M:

The biggest key to accelerating your agency revenues to $1M is to increase your prices and sell high-ticket items. The higher the price, the less services you will have to sell. Now, this will mean increasing the quality of your services so that the customer will see enough value to justify the price. But the better the quality you provide, the more the word of mouth will cause your reputation to grow.

Also, agencies are people-heavy. Therefore, the more you can productize, systematize, and automate your business operations, the faster you can scale your business to $1M or more.

Suping Up Your Vehicle with Accelerators

But remember, your business model is just one piece of the puzzle. To truly accelerate your success, you'll want to incorporate some general "100X Accelerators."

Combined with your business model, these battle-tested techniques can be your secret weapon on the path to $1M.

Here are a few of the accelerators you can add to your business model that will help you get to your $1M goal quicker and easier:

Capitalize on Hot Trends

Find a hot trend and add it to your business model in some way, either through content creation or a product add-on. Because of the high demand caused by the trend, people will come to you also because they will see you as a trusted authority in this field.

Dominate a Micro-Niche

A niche is a microcosm of people who have similar values and needs. A micro niche is an even smaller subset of people with similar values whose needs are not being met because they are a smaller group.

This leaves a gap in the marketplace for those willing to create solutions for these people. Also, many people in micro niches are eager to pay high prices because of the scarcity of service providers available to solve their problems.

Build a Rabid Audience

Building an audience of superfans will provide you with a great community to buy your products and services and test new ones. Your superfans can quickly become your brand ambassadors, spreading the news about your products and services and helping them go viral.

Combining the right business model with these powerful growth accelerators will make you unstoppable on your $1M journey.

For example, when I began my publishing company, the video game Minecraft had just come out. Minecraft was trending globally, creating a massive demand for video game fanfiction. Since very few people were serving this micro-niche audience, I decided to make Minecraft kids' books the first line of books we would create. Our books were such a hit that they went global in only a few months and allowed us to sell millions of copies, even in an environment where most authors barely sell one thousand copies.

That is the power of using 100X accelerators.

So, Which Business Model Are You Going to Choose?

So, which business model is calling your name? Which one makes your entrepreneurial heart beat just a little bit faster?

Trust your instincts, but also do your homework.

To become more familiar with these business models, watch YouTube videos, read case studies, read books, learn from experts, and start testing and validating your ideas.

Remember, the path to $1M is not a straight line. It's a winding road filled with pivots, detours, and unexpected opportunities. The business model you start with may be different from the one that ultimately takes you to the top. But by staying flexible, adaptable, and relentlessly focused on providing value, you can navigate any twist and turn on the road to 7-figure success.

Conclusion: It's Time to Choose Your $1M Vehicle

Wow, what a ride! We've explored ten incredible business models, each a unique and powerful vehicle for your $1M journey. From the sleek lines of Affiliate Marketing to the rugged power of Service Businesses, from the eco-friendly efficiency of SaaS to the spacious luxury of Information Products, you now have a better understanding of the top entrepreneurial rides on the market.

But this is just the beginning of your adventure. Choosing your business model is like selecting your car—it's a critical decision. Still, it's what you do with it that really counts. The real excitement begins when you turn the key, step on the gas, and start navigating the twists and turns of your entrepreneurial journey.

So, if you are ready, let's get started.

ACTION STEPS

1. Pick the business model from this list you will pursue for the next 90 Days.

2. Watch 10-20 YouTube Videos on that business model until you feel like you understand how the rules work for that model.

If you want more proven systems to help you make your first million faster, join the 100X Entrepreneur's Club for FREE today: **100xClub.ai**.

Chapter 5

FINDING YOUR DREAM CUSTOMER

Have you ever wondered why in the world you would want to get involved with crazy customers? Or have you ever dreaded the idea of meeting with customers or even calling them?

When I first started in business, I was so desperate that I took any and every warm body that would be willing to pay me to be a customer.

The result? I was miserable.

You see, I couldn't stand some of my customers, and I didn't like the others very much either, which made it almost impossible to meet their needs. Why? Because customers are needy. And in business, your entire job is to meet their needs.

So when customers called or complained, all I could hear were nails dragging on a chalkboard.

It got so bad in one of my businesses that I eventually let it die. This was a 20-million-dollar business, mind you. But I let it die because no matter how much I tried, I couldn't connect with my customers. They weren't bad; I just wasn't passionate about serving them.

In my other business, though, I fell in love with my customers. I loved serving them so much that I loved talking to them daily, hearing about their needs, and even hearing their complaints because it gave me the opportunity to create even better products for them.

And not only did I make $25-30 million with that business, but that business is still going strong today.

The biggest lesson I learned from this entire experience was the importance of finding your dream customer.

Finding Your Dream Customer

"If you try to help everyone, you will end up helping no one." This simple yet profound truth is the key to unlocking your entrepreneurial journey's most significant growth and fulfillment potential.

Even Superman couldn't save everyone. But the one person he always saved was Lois Lane. In the same way, you need to focus your energy on serving the customers who ignite your passion and align with your purpose.

As I mentioned, when I started my business, I struggled to attract customers. Out of desperation, I took on any client I could get, only to find myself dreading the work and resenting the very people I was meant to serve.

But then I realized that if I focused on serving customers I truly cared about and solving problems that deeply mattered to me, I could build a business that not only generated millions but also fueled my soul.

By becoming a champion for my dream customers and obsessing over solving their most painful problems, I tapped into a wellspring of creativity, energy, and unstoppable motivation.

I went above and beyond, constantly innovating and improving my offerings and forging deep partnerships with my customers. As I poured my heart into serving them, they rewarded me with their loyalty, referrals, and ever-growing investment in my products and services.

In this chapter, we'll journey to help you identify your dream customer and uncover the million-dollar problem you're uniquely positioned to solve.

This is the foundation upon which your entire business will be built, and it's the secret to creating a 7-figure enterprise that will fill you with pride and purpose.

The Anatomy of a Dream Customer

Before we identify your ideal customer, let's consider the key characteristics of a dream customer for a $1M business.

A dream customer is:

1. A customer you genuinely want to serve.

This is someone whose success and happiness truly matter to you and for whom you're willing to go the extra mile.

2. Has a problem you're passionate about solving.

The challenge they face is one that you're uniquely equipped and excited to tackle and that aligns with your values and vision.

3. Has the ability to pay.

Your dream customer must have the financial means to invest in your solution, ensuring you can build a profitable and sustainable business.

And not just on the smaller end, but your dream customer must be able to afford your higher-end products and services as well.

4. Is in a growing market.

Ideally, your dream customer is part of a larger, expanding market that provides ample opportunity for growth and scale.

5. Bonus—Is in a trending market.

If your dream customer and their problem are part of a current hot trend, you can ride the wave of momentum and interest to accelerate your results.

I must admit that when I built my children's publishing company, I was not interested in serving kids. I just wanted to sell a product and make money.

But things changed. As I started writing for these kids, the overwhelming response from both kids and parents changed me. Parents spoke of how their children hated reading until they read my books and learned to love reading. The kids would share how much the books helped them overcome the biggest challenges of their preteen lives. So, after hearing thousands of these responses, I became a champion for these kids, and we've written 45 of these books and are still going strong to this day.

My new dream customers also met all five of the dream customer criteria perfectly, which led to the sale of millions of copies of our books.

 Reflection Exercise

1. Who would you say is your dream customer that you want to be a champion for?

2. What problems are you passionate about solving? Who else would benefit from you solving this problem?

3. What customer would you be excited to wake up and help every day?

Finding Your Million-Dollar Problem to Solve

Once you've identified your dream customer, the next step is to zero in on the problem they face that you're destined to solve.

But not all problems are created equal—some are too small, too easily solved by others, or simply not profitable enough to build a $1M business.

Therefore, to find your million-dollar problem, you'll need to start by listing all your dream customers pain points, then asking yourself these 7 Key Problem Criteria Questions:

1. Is it truly a meaningful problem for you and your dream customer?
2. Is it a widespread problem faced by a significant number of people?
3. Is it currently underserved by existing solutions?
4. Are enough people willing to pay to solve this problem?
5. Is the problem part of a growing trend or an expanding market?
6. Is it a recurring problem that customers need to solve repeatedly?
7. Can you solve this problem better than anyone else?

When you find a problem that meets all these criteria, you've struck gold. This is the foundation for a business that has the potential to generate millions and one that you'll be intrinsically motivated to grow and scale.

For example, when I sold binoculars, I decided to read the thousands of reviews we had gotten for the past few years to see if there were ways that I could serve my customers better. What I found was a consistent complaint among birdwatchers that binoculars needed to be designed with them in mind (hunters buy 90% of binoculars). With this information, I researched what birdwatchers needed in binoculars; then, I asked my manufacturer to change our specifications to be precisely what the birdwatchers were clamoring for.

From then on out, our birdwatching binocular company was born, and within the first year, I made my first $1M in a month.

Where to Find Million-Dollar Problems to Solve

But how do you find these million-dollar problems? Here are a few strategies:

1. Ask your dream customers directly what their main problems are. You can interview them directly or use surveys or focus groups.
2. Look at your own challenges and frustrations—chances are, others face similar issues.
3. Study bestseller lists and marketplaces to see what solutions are in high demand.
4. Analyze search engine queries and trends to uncover common pain points.
5. Leverage AI tools like ChatGPT to generate problem ideas and insights.

Remember, your goal isn't just to find a problem—it's to find a problem that is meaningful to your dream customer and that you're uniquely positioned and passionate about solving. This is the key to building a business that generates wealth and fulfills your deeper purpose and potential.

Accelerating Your Success

As you embark on this journey of discovering your dream customer and their million-dollar problem, there are a few key strategies that can help accelerate your success:

1. Look for trending problems.
For example, as of the writing of this book, you can find trending problems in emerging fields like AI, virtual reality, or blockchain.

2. Identify bestselling products or services and find ways to improve them.
For example, look at bestselling products and read their 2–3-star reviews. Then, produce similar products but improve on the areas customers complained about. Then, tell them how your product does what the others don't.

3. Dive deep into a micro-niche where you can become the go-to expert and authority.
For example, plenty of subcategories of popular niches are not being served. I mentioned how I created Minecraft fan fiction. It was a subcategory of a niche (Minecraft) with great demand, but very few service providers were willing to serve this micro-niche. I decided to champion this micro-niche, and the rest is history.

By combining these strategies with a relentless focus on your dream customer and their most pressing problem, you'll be well on your way to building a 7-figure business that fuels your passion and transforms your life.

 Reflection Exercise

Let's take a moment to put this all into practice.

1. Open a fresh document and start brainstorming your potential dream customers.

2. Who are the people you feel most called to serve? What are their characteristics, values, goals, and challenges?

3. Next, start listing out the problems they face that you are uniquely positioned and passionate to solve.

4. Cross-reference these problems against the 7 Key Problem Criteria Questions to ensure they have the potential to support a $1M business.

5. Finally, choose the customer and problem pair that ignites your excitement and aligns with your vision.

6. This will be your North Star, the guiding light that will illuminate your path to seven-figure success.

Conclusion: Your Fuel and Focus

The journey ahead won't always be easy. Still, with your dream customer and their million-dollar problem as fuel and focus, you can overcome any obstacle and achieve the impossible.

Remember, this isn't just about finding any old customer or solving any old problem. It's about finding your perfect match, the one that makes you excited about waking up in the morning and getting to work.

It's about falling in love with serving them, becoming their hero and champion, and making their success and happiness your ultimate mission and reward.

So, as you turn the page on this chapter, know that you're not just starting a business—you're embarking on a partnership. A partnership between you and your dream customers, your unique gifts, and the problems you were born to solve. A partnership that has the power to change lives, create incredible value, and build a legacy of impact and abundance.

The road ahead won't always be easy, but with the clarity and conviction you've gained from this chapter, you have everything you need to make your $1M a reality. So take a deep breath, trust in your newfound wisdom, and take that first step towards finding and serving your dream customer like no one else can.

ACTION STEPS

1. Pick the dream customer that you will be a champion for these next 90 days.

2. Talk to 3 of your dream customers and interview them so that you can understand their pain points.

3. Pick 1 of your dream customer's pain points and devote yourself to solving it for the next 90 days.

If you want more proven systems to help you make your first million faster, join the 100X Entrepreneur's Club for FREE today: **100xClub.ai**.

Chapter 6

CRAFTING THE PERFECT SOLUTION FOR YOUR DREAM CUSTOMER

You've found your dream customer, and you've uncovered the million-dollar problem that's keeping them up at night. Congrats! You're halfway to entrepreneurial success.

But now comes the hard part: actually solving that problem in a way that delights your customer and fills your bank account.

In a perfect world, every solution you create for your dream customer would be welcomed with open arms and open wallets. But the reality is that, like a clueless husband, you're going to do a lot of things and have little idea what makes your wife (customer) happy.

Now, the smart husband will keep trying over and over again. But the genius husband would simply ask his wife what she wants and give it to her.

For the longest time, finding solutions for my dream customer was expensive trial and error. I kept trying new ideas over and over again in the hopes that I would eventually find something that my dream customers would like.

But then I eventually learned that if I just interviewed my dream customers and found out what they liked, it would give me an excellent starting point for creating products and services they would happily pay for.

Finding the Ideal Solution for Your Dream Customer

So, if you're like most entrepreneurs, you're probably swimming in a sea of doubt and uncertainty right now. How do you create a solution that truly meets your customer's needs? How do you stand out in a crowded market full of competitors? And how the heck do you get your solution into the hands of more than just a handful of people?

First, take a deep breath. You've got this. As an entrepreneur, finding solutions is what you were born to do. It's in your DNA, your very essence. And when you devote yourself to solving your dream customer's problems better than anyone else, you're not just building a business—you're creating an impact.

But let's be real: not all solutions are created equal. The perfect solution isn't just about solving the problem—it's about creating a win-win scenario for both you and your customer.

So, how do you create the ideal solution for your dream customer's problem? Fear not—we've got you covered. In this chapter, we'll be diving deep into the art and science of solution crafting. You'll learn the secret formula for creating an offer that checks all the boxes, from effectiveness and user-friendliness to profitability and scalability.

The 100X Solution Creation Criteria: Your Key to a Win-Win Offer

At the heart of every perfect solution is a set of criteria ensuring a smashing success for you and your customer. We call this the 100X Solution Creation Criteria, and it's your ticket to finding a solution that your dream customer will love.

To create an offer that truly shines, your solution must:

1. Solve your dream customer's problem effectively and efficiently.
Your solution should help your dream customer achieve their desired outcome with the least time, effort, sacrifice, and risk possible.

2. Be user-friendly and easy to adopt.
Your solution should be intuitive, accessible, and a joy to use. Bonus points if it's so remarkable that your customers can't stop raving about it to their friends.

3. Provide a delightful user experience.
Your solution shouldn't just solve the problem—it should make your customer's life better, easier, and more enjoyable.

4. Be profitable for you to deliver.
Your solution is only sustainable if it allows you to generate a healthy profit margin. Remember to factor in all your costs, from development to marketing to customer support.

5. Be easily scalable to the masses.

Your solution should be designed to be easily delivered to many customers without costing a fortune or burning yourself out.

6. Make it unique and differentiated.

Your solution should stand out from the competition and offer a fresh, innovative approach to solving your customer's problem.

7. Create scarcity and exclusivity.

The rarer and more exclusive your solution feels, the more irresistible it becomes to your dream customers.

8. Build a competitive advantage.

Look for ways to make your solution difficult to copy or reverse-engineer, whether through proprietary technology, exclusive partnerships, or a strong brand identity.

By designing your solution with these criteria in mind, you'll be well on your way to creating an offer that your dream customers can't resist and your competitors can't touch.

Our birdwatching binoculars fit every one of these criteria for our dream customers. From solving the customer's problem effectively to being user-friendly, enjoyable to use, unique and differentiated, and even having a strong competitive advantage, they checked all the boxes. Because of this, our company became the global brand for birdwatching binoculars in as little as two years.

ChatGPT is another product that checks all these boxes very well. And this explains its rapid global expansion in such a short period of time.

Delivering Your Solution Like a Boss

But crafting the perfect solution is only half the battle. To really make your solution sing, you need to deliver it in a way that's both easy for your customers to access and profitable for you to provide.

This means choosing delivery methods that allow you to reach the widest possible audience within your dream customer base while also minimizing your own time, effort, and expense.

Whether it's an online course, a mobile app, or a physical product, your delivery strategy should be carefully designed to maximize your impact and income.

So, how do you go about designing this picture-perfect solution? Here are a few key strategies:

1. Ask your dream customers directly.
Conduct surveys, interviews, and focus groups to get inside their heads and understand precisely what they want and need from a solution and how they want it delivered.

2. Study your competitors and look for ways to improve.
Analyze customer reviews, identify gaps in the market, and brainstorm ways to differentiate your offer. See how your competition is delivering the solution and do it better.

3. Leverage proven business models and best practices.
Study what's already working in your industry and adapt it to your unique vision.

4. Test, test, and test some more.

Launch a beta version of your solution and gather feedback from real customers. Then, update and improve based on their input.

 Reflection Exercise

1. Pick 3-5 possible solutions for your dream customer's main pain point.
2. Modify these solutions using 100X Solution Creation Criteria.
3. Brainstorm how you can deliver the solution to your dream customers in a way that is convenient for them and low cost for you.

Remember, crafting the perfect solution is an ongoing process. As your dream customers' needs evolve and new technologies emerge, you must continually refine and update your offer to stay ahead of the curve.

But with the 100X Solution Creation Criteria as your guide and a relentless focus on delivering value to your customers, you'll be well-equipped to build a business that stands the test of time.

Conclusion: A Solution Your Dream Customers Will Adore

We've covered a lot of ground in this chapter. From the key criteria of a winning solution to the strategies for designing and delivering your offer, you now have a comprehensive blueprint for crafting a product or service that your dream customers will adore.

But don't just take our word for it. It's time to put these principles into action. Look at the problem you've identified for your dream customer and start brainstorming potential solutions. Run each idea through the 100X Solution Creation Criteria and see how it stacks up. Then, start contacting your dream customers and gathering their feedback and insights.

Remember, the path to the perfect solution is paved with experimentation, iteration, and a whole lot of customer love. Don't be afraid to try new things, pivot when necessary, and always keep your dream customer's needs at the forefront of your mind.

ACTION STEPS

1. Choose three solutions that will solve your Dream customer's problem that you are trying to solve.

2. Talk to your dream customers and see which one they love most.

3. After talking to them, choose one solution you will focus on for the next 90 days.

If you want more proven systems to help you make your first million faster, join the 100X Entrepreneur's Club for FREE today: **100xClub.ai**.

Chapter 7

VALIDATING YOUR MILLION-DOLLAR IDEA IN THE REAL WORLD

I don't know if you can relate, but at different times, I have been so discouraged in my entrepreneurial journey that I've wanted to give up and get a regular job.

When I first started, I felt frustrated most of the time. I mean, I would get an idea, then immediately get my domain, logo, and LLC, put the product or service together, open for business, and then wait for people to show up.

But, again and again, the result was the same. No one would show up, and no one would buy.

Then, I'd create an expensive website and spend a lot of money on ads. But again, no buyers.

I'm stubborn, so I would try again, again and again. Until I got so discouraged that I threw my hands up in frustration. I was about to quit entrepreneurship and get a job.

Luckily, I saw an interview with Tim Ferris, who was interviewing Noah Kagan. And Noah said a few words that changed my life forever:

"Before you build or spend money on anything, find a cheap way to find out if anyone even wants what you have to offer. And the cheapest way to do that is to sell it before you make it."

What he said changed the way I operated my business forever.

From then on, before spending a dime on domains, websites, ads, LLCs, or even building my product, I would first test to see if anyone would pay for the magic of my idea, even before I made it.

I got my first taste of the powerful world of validation.

The Role of Validation in Your Entrepreneurial Journey

Think about it. You come up with what you believe is the perfect solution for your dream customer's problem. But how do you know if anyone else wants or cares about it?

The problem is that the market can be fickle, and it's hard to predict what people will want. Even if people say they like your idea, it doesn't mean much unless they are willing to pay.

So, how do you ensure that your dream customer wants the solution you offer before spending all the time, effort, resources, and money building it?

Like Noah said: "sell it before you make it."

If you can create an offer that people are desperate to buy, even before you've built the product or service, you've struck business gold. Because when your solution finally comes out, it will sell itself, you'll spend less on marketing, and you'll be able to charge premium prices.

The Nitty-Gritty of Validation: Tactics and Strategies

This is known as validation, or product-market fit, which confirms that there is a large market eager to buy what you're offering, even before you create it.

Validation is so important that it's like putting the key into your business's ignition. Without validation, you get the clickety-click of a car that won't start. But when you have validation, the engine roars to life.

Therefore, here are a few simple, inexpensive, yet effective tactics you can use to validate your business idea, even before you build it:

1. Talk to dream customers in person and try to sell them on your idea. Since you are already meeting up with your potential dream customers to understand their pain points and get feedback on possible solutions, use the opportunity to make them an offer on the spot.

If they say no, ask them why, and keep working on your solution until they say yes.

2. Email or text people you know, offering them your solution.

Create a simple email, text, or social media post describing your product's benefits, adding a payment link and offering a discount. Then, send the email, text, or post to your dream customers to see if they will buy your solution. If you start making sales, you know you're on the right track.

3. Post about it in online groups or forums where your dream customer hangs out.

Join online groups full of your dream customers and serve them for a few weeks. Then, let them know about your offer to see if anyone would be interested. Just make sure this is allowed in the group or offer a free trial so that it won't be an issue.

4. Create a simple Google or Facebook ad and send traffic to your landing page to test if people will buy.

Create a simple landing page with your solution, its benefits, and a payment link. Then, send ad traffic to it to see how people respond. If they respond, great. If not, try again and again with a different solution until it is validated.

5. Set up a crowdfunding campaign on a platform like Kickstarter or Indiegogo.

Crowdfunding campaigns are great for raising money and validating whether people want your product or service. If your campaign becomes popular, you will also attract the attention of major funders who see the proven demand for your product or service.

6. Create a waiting list and collect deposits from interested customers.
Sometimes, it can be difficult to sell your product or service before you make it (E.g., SaaS or mobile apps). Therefore, the next best thing is to create a waiting list for those who want to be the first to try it. To motivate them to jump on board, offer them a discount or a bonus for being early adopters of your solution. You can even ask them for a small deposit.

The biggest benefit of a waiting list is that once you launch, many people will be ready to buy your product.

7. Make a simple prototype or mockup and ask people to pre-order the final product.
Another option is to create a digital mockup, animation, presentation, video, or Figma to help describe your product or service. Sometimes, that is all you need to convince people to buy it or put a deposit on it. These options still convey the magic of your solution while keeping your spending to a minimum.

8. Conduct surveys and gather feedback from your dream customers.
While not the ideal solution, conducting surveys and gathering feedback gives you insights into the desires of your dream customers. Though it won't guarantee that your dream customers will buy your solution, it will at least increase the odds that they will.

One of the best validation strategies I have ever used as an author was to presell a book cover before I wrote the book. Writing a book takes a lot of time and effort. So, normally, you would only find out if anyone liked your book after you've put in the painstaking effort of writing it. And most of the time, they wouldn't like it.

I discovered I could get a book cover made for $10 and then list it for presale on Amazon Advantage. If 100+ people bought it in a 30-day period, it would validate my idea, and then I would write the book. If not, I would cancel the presale.

One of my biggest successes with this strategy was a book cover that sold 900 copies even before I wrote the book. When I finally wrote the book, I made over six figures on that one book alone in a span of 12 months.

Criteria for Successful Validation

How many sales do you need to consider your idea validated?

Selling too little during the presale phase can give you a false sense of validation. Therefore, it is good to have a rule of thumb to ensure you have a product the market wants.

From my experience validating hundreds of products and services, here are some good rules of thumb to aim for:

1. First Validation: 5+ sales in 1-2 weeks

The first validation is to see if there is interest in what you have to offer. Five or more sales in a span of one to two weeks is a good sign that you may have a successful solution.

2. Second Validation: 50+ sales in 30-45 days

Ideally, a successful product or service increases sales over time. After your first validation, you should expect to sell more products and services faster as more people hear about it.

50+ sales within a 30–45-day period (daily sales) are good indicators that you have a successful product.

3. Third Validation: 500+ sales in 3-4 months (this is considered true product-market fit)

The third validation is the most important because it will truly reveal whether your solution has high market demand and if you've achieved product market fit.

For validation to occur, your sales should be growing consistently over time. Therefore, 500+ sales in a 3–4 month period is a good indicator that you have a solution the market wants and that you can build a thriving business on.

Does Price Affect the Validation Period?

You may wonder whether price affects the validation rules of thumb I just mentioned.

The answer is yes but to a degree.

For example, for lower-priced products (under $500), you can use the validation rules of thumb from the previous list.

Validation may take twice as long for higher-priced products because of the limited number of target customers who can afford high prices.

However, the same principles apply: You need to show increasing sales to truly confirm that you have achieved product market fit.

How To Price During the Validation Period

When pricing products or services during the validation period, you want to motivate your dream customers to buy.

One way to do this is to offer a bonus for signing up early. Or you can offer your product at a 50% discount. Another option, especially for subscription-based services, is to offer your product with lifetime access as a bonus for signing up early.

Other Validation Considerations

During validation, you want to keep your expenses low, spending at most $50-$100 per offer for low-ticket items to cover costs and marketing. You can go as high as $500-$1000 for high-ticket items. However, the key is not to spend more than the price of one of the items you are promoting. This way, if you sell 3+ items, you will have already covered your cost and earned a profit. But if you don't sell much, you don't lose much.

Before you see validation, you want to avoid spending money on domains, branding, ads, and legal structure. After the first valida-tion, you can spend money on a domain name. After the second validation, you can spend money on ads and branding, and after the third validation (product-market fit), you can consider spending money on a legal entity.

But what do you do if your idea doesn't get validated?

Keep going. Simply drop it and move on to testing something else. There are thousands of potentially irresistible solutions out there that the market wants. You need to keep putting out as many offers as possible until you catch something.

I thank Noah Kagan for introducing this concept to me over a decade ago. In the interview with Tim Ferris, by saying we are not in the business of building businesses but testing businesses, all the pressure of building and succeeding at business went away.

I realized now that I could fail a lot, and it wouldn't mean much because I was only testing. Also, my expectations became more realistic, understanding that 90% of my ideas would fail. This motivated me to test and fail as quickly as possible to find the 10% of ideas that would succeed.

And eventually, I succeeded at building two eight-figure businesses and another six-figure business that became a cash cow for me. But that was after testing multiple other business ideas that never saw the light of day.

 Reflection Exercise

1. What business idea do you have that you would like to validate?

2. Create a text or email with a payment link and send it to a few dream customers right now.

3. If you get five sales, it's validated. If not, try another idea, then another.

Conclusion: Validation, Your Business Superpower

Validation is the key to ensuring your business idea is viable, profitable, and scalable. Use tactics like selling before you build, talking to customers directly, leveraging online communities, establishing a waiting list, and setting up test campaigns to gather real-world feedback on your idea.

Aim for concrete sales goals to confirm validation and be prepared to update your idea based on the feedback you receive. Remember, the worst thing that can happen is not that people reject your idea but that you never put it out there in the first place.

Embrace the validation process as the key to unlocking your entrepreneurial success. Put your million-dollar idea to the test, and let the market be your guide. With validation, you'll have the green light to turn your dream into a thriving, profitable reality.

ACTION STEPS

1. **Send an offer to 10-20 of your dream customers (via text, email, social media post, or in person).**

   - If five buy, it is validated.

   - If five do not buy, choose a different solution, and send out a new offer.

   - Keep doing this until one of your ideas is validated.

If you want more proven systems to help you make your first million faster, join the 100X Entrepreneur's Club for FREE today: **100xClub.ai**.

Chapter 8

THE 80/20 MARKETING STRATEGY

Hurray! You've managed to get a few people to buy your product!

Now, you may be wondering how to reach everyone else who might want it. You might wonder whether those initial sales were real or just a fluke. You may also be overwhelmed by the idea of getting your message out there, especially if you're an introvert or have a small network.

Welcome to the world of marketing.

But think about this for a moment. Has this ever happened to you?

Someone tells you that if you want to market your services, you must spend money on ads. Then, you spend a ton of money on ads.

Then, someone tells you, that you must create content on social media. So, you spend a ton of effort creating content on social media.

Then someone says you need a website, landing page, and email provider to build your list, so you spend a lot of time and money on them.

Then, after a few months, you look at all your results, and you have very little to show for your efforts, except for an empty bank account.

If this has ever happened to you, and you're scratching your head about it like I was, I want to let you in on a little secret.

Your marketing didn't work because it was bad—it didn't work because your timing was bad.

Let me explain by introducing you to the 80/20 Marketing Strategy.

The 80/20 Marketing Strategy

Marketing is the effort you make to make more of your dream customers aware of your solution.

I'm sure you have heard of all types of marketing tactics, from social media to running ads to SEO, etc. And you're probably overwhelmed by the vast number of options for marketing your solution.

I am here to tell you that if you want to reach more of your dream customers, you need to focus most of your attention and resources on the most vital few marketing tactics first and everything else second.

Meaning you need to work smarter, not harder.

Here's what I mean.

The truth is that not all marketing efforts are created equal. The 80/20 principle tells us that 80% of your marketing results will come from just 20% of your marketing efforts, while the remaining 80% will only generate 20% of your results.

Therefore, the key to successful marketing is to focus most of your time and energy on the top 20% of marketing activities that deliver the most significant impact.

Think of marketing like investing. If you put all your money into safe, stable investments, your wealth will grow slowly and incrementally over time, which is nice. But with inflation eating away at your returns, that slow and steady approach alone isn't enough to get ahead. To really supercharge your growth, you need to allocate a portion of your resources to investments with exponential potential.

An 80/20 Marketing Strategy applies this same principle to your marketing efforts. It involves dividing your marketing activities into two tiers:

1. Incremental Marketing (The Bottom 80%)
Incremental marketing are efforts that generates small, consistent returns over time. Though useful, because of the small returns,

incremental marketing efforts are not where you should spend most of your time, energy, and resources.

2. Exponential Marketing (The Top 20%)

Exponential marketing efforts, on the other hand, are activities that have the potential to generate 10X returns from your marketing in a very short period of time. Therefore, because of the outsized returns you get from exponential marketing, this is where you want to focus the majority of your resources.

The key is to strike the right balance between these two tiers while dedicating the lion's share of your time and resources to exponential marketing activities.

Incremental Marketing: The Slow and Steady Foundation

Incremental Marketing efforts are efforts that you make that bring small, incremental results over time. The truth is that most of your marketing results will come from small incremental growth over time. Yet, because of their small and slow returns, you cannot focus your valuable time and effort on them.

Incremental marketing includes tactics like:

1. Reaching out to prospects one at a time.
2. Content marketing strategies like posting on social media, blogging or SEO article writing.
3. Developing an email list and nurturing those subscribers over time.
4. Cold calling, cold direct messaging (DM), or cold emailing potential customers.

5. Running ads (Google, Facebook, LinkedIn).
6. Regular networking at industry events.
7. Search engine optimization (SEO) to improve your website's organic ranking gradually.

These activities are essential for building a solid marketing foundation and establishing your brand's presence over the long term. However, they tend to generate returns slowly, often taking years to bear fruit.

The key to success with incremental tactics is to automate, delegate, or simplify these marketing tactics as much as possible. Use technology to automate and streamline your processes, outsource tasks to skilled professionals, and look for ways to achieve similar results with less time and effort.

The ultimate goal is to keep these activities ticking along in the background without letting them consume the bulk of your resources.

For example, recently, I started building my personal brand on social media channels, specifically focusing on building my audience. Because it relies so heavily on constant posting on social media, it takes a lot of my time and effort to produce the large amount of content that is required.

So, I decided to train an AI agent to produce high-quality content for me and write in my voice. Now, 90% of my social media is run by AI, and I only spend a few minutes weekly improving the quality of the content and checking on the progress.

What is humbling is that I got more followers and engagement from the AI-generated posts I put out than from the ones I created from scratch myself.

Exponential Marketing: The High-Octane Growth Engine

Exponential marketing efforts are marketing tactics that can generate massive returns in a compressed timeframe, often delivering 10X or even 100X results.

The ROI for exponential marketing efforts is so significant that it can quickly add many zeros to your profits. Because of this, exponential marketing is where you need to focus the bulk of your valuable time, effort, and resources.

Here is a list of the most impactful exponential marketing efforts in business:

1. Reaching Out to Current Customers

- Upselling or cross-selling to your current customer base allows you to create more lifetime value per customer. Since they already know you and trust you, they are the lowest-hanging fruit that can quickly make you more sales.
- Developing a systemized referral program to turn customers into brand evangelists is another low-hanging fruit tactic that leads to high-quality sales. Great customers hang out with other great customers, so if you proactively ask for referrals, they will bring you high-quality customers who will spend as they do.

2. Dream 100 Targeting

- Identifying and targeting the top 100 ideal dream customers you'd love to work with will allow you to eventually acquire some of your industry's highest-quality customers. Though it will take time, you can relentlessly pursue and acquire those "whale" accounts through personalized outreach and adding value.
- Building relationships with the 100 most influential people in your space through consistent, targeted engagement will also open massive opportunities to serve millions more of your dream customers.

3. Influencer Marketing

- Partnering with influencers who have already built audiences that overlap with your target market can give you access to thousands and even millions more of your dream customers.
- This means leveraging the clout of nano, micro, and macro influencers to expand your reach exponentially.

4. Community Building (aka Group Marketing)

- Embedding yourself in online or offline communities filled with your ideal customers and serving them will increase your influence among your dream customers.
- By offering massive value, consistently helping others, and sharing your expertise, you will quickly build authority and land more customers.

5. Strategic Partnerships

- Forging alliances with non-competing businesses that serve the same customer base is another way to reach many of your dream customers quickly.
- This can be done through developing co-marketing campaigns or joint venture projects that provide massive exposure.

6. Trendjacking

- Aligning your content marketing with hot trends and buzzy topics in your industry can quickly attract more people to you.
- Newsjacking relevant current events or piggybacking on viral memes to boost your brand's visibility and quickly build awareness of your brand.

7. Affiliate Armies

- Building a network of commission-based affiliates incentivized to promote your product will multiply your outreach.
- Equipping affiliates with the tools, training, and resources they need will make generating massive results easier for these sales armies.

8. Guest Speaking on Stages and Panels

- Securing speaking engagements at high-profile industry events attended by your target audience makes you an authority and rapidly increases your influence with your dream customers.

- Guest speaking on popular podcasts, webinars, or virtual summits to gain trust and expand your reach is another way to quickly build your influence.

These exponential tactics require more upfront effort to set in motion, but they have the potential to unlock rapid, exponential growth. The key is to focus on high-leverage activities that put you in front of the right people and allow you to make a big splash quickly.

For example, by establishing a strategic partnership with Scholastic, the global leader in children's books, I was able to quickly distribute our Minecraft fanfiction books to all parts of the world. This partnership opened massive access to global markets and gave our books instant credibility because they were endorsed by the biggest name in children's books.

 Reflection Exercise

1. Going through the list of exponential and incremental marketing efforts, which ones are you spending the most time on (incremental or exponential)?

2. If you're focusing on the wrong areas, rearrange your focus and put it where it will have the greatest impact.

Accelerating Your Exponential Plays and Automating Your Incremental Ones

To truly accelerate your exponential and incremental marketing efforts, consider implementing some 100X accelerators. These strategies can help you achieve 10X marketing results with 10X less time and effort.

For example, one powerful way to accelerate your Exponential Marketing is to identify groups full of influencers and potential strategic partners and become involved in them instead of reaching out to influencers one at a time. By connecting with groups full of high-level influencers in your industry, you can reach many of them more quickly and build instant trust with them because of your affiliation with the group.

The key here is to focus on both the quality and quantity of these groups. Look for groups full of influencers who specifically cater to your dream customer.

Sometimes, it will cost you money to be involved in these groups, but the return on investment is so high that you will recoup, even 10X your investment, very quickly.

Another powerful accelerator is to create a viral loop in your marketing campaigns, where each new user brings in multiple new users through referrals or social sharing. You can also leverage user-generated content, such as customer reviews or social media posts, to build trust and credibility with your audience.

On the other hand, to accelerate your Incremental Marketing efforts, consistently grow a massive audience by creating valuable content and engaging with your target audience. This means posting on social media multiple times daily and actively participating in relevant conversations.

Tools like AI and automation software can help automate tasks, such as generating content, scheduling social media posts, and managing email marketing campaigns.

Conclusion: 80/20 Marketing for Maximum Impact

Ultimately, the 80/20 Marketing Strategy aims to help you allocate your time and resources for maximum impact. By automating your incremental activities and doubling down on your exponential plays, you can achieve explosive growth and reach your $1M goal faster.

But this isn't just about tactics and techniques. It's about adopting an exponential mindset and being willing to take bold, decisive action to achieve outsized results.

It's about recognizing that not all marketing activities are created equal and being ruthless about prioritizing the 20% of efforts that will generate 80% of your returns.

It's about focusing on the big, automating the small, and scaling quickly—leveraging the power of this combination to expand your reach.

So, as you craft your own 80/20 Marketing Strategy, remember that fortune favors the bold. Don't be afraid to think differently, act decisively, and pursue exponential growth with everything you've got.

ACTION STEPS

1. Exponential

- Set up your Dream 100 Customers and Influencers list, then start reaching out to your Dream 100 customers and influencers.

2. Incremental

- Pick the incremental marketing efforts you will use, then begin to automate, delegate, or simplify them so they will be consistently done, with little of your time and effort.

If you want more proven systems to help you make your first million faster, join the 100X Entrepreneur's Club for FREE today: **100xClub.ai**.

Chapter 9

THE ART AND SCIENCE OF IRRESISTIBLE OFFERS AND SALES

Ever since I was younger, I had problems finding a girlfriend. Even if I found a girl that liked me, I would open my mouth, and they would run for the hills.

The sad thing is that, for some reason, that same experience also followed me into the business world.

For example, in business, I was so bad at sales that I couldn't give my stuff away for free. I would discount my services to the point that I was paying my customers to take my business, and they would still say no.

The biggest reason I was such a terrible salesperson was that I was too desperate to get people to buy. People could sense my desperation as I pushed my products onto people.

You see, sales was something I did TO people instead of FOR people. And as customers sensed this, they didn't want anything to do with it.

Eventually, I realized that sales had nothing to do with me but everything to do with the customer. I realized that the customer had a problem, and I had the solution for that problem. I just had to help them come to that conclusion on their own.

Once I started focusing on my customers and solving their problems, my sales went from being embarrassingly dismal to a closing ratio of 92%, closing anyone sitting in front of me. I could do the same thing from the stage as well.

The surprisingly good news is that it worked in my personal life as well. I found the woman of my dreams, and I married her. Later, I found out it wasn't because of my fantastic sales skills that she married me. Instead, my wife was a natural-born saleswoman in her own right, and she convinced me to gladly make the biggest purchase of my life—a diamond ring.

Mastering the Art of Selling

Selling can be a steep challenge for many entrepreneurs. The fear of sounding "salesy," uncertainty about pricing, and difficulty communicating value can all prevent entrepreneurs from making the sales their business needs to thrive.

If any of this sounds familiar, you're not alone. Many entrepreneurs struggle with sales because they have yet to learn how to craft irresistible offers and communicate value effectively.

But here's the good news: if you've done your homework by identifying your dream customer, creating a solution they desperately want, and validating market demand, then selling becomes infinitely easier.

With the right offer and messaging, your product or service can practically sell itself.

The Value/Price Seesaw: Finding the Sweet Spot

Imagine a seesaw with value on one end and price on the other. The key to making sales effortless is to load up the value side of the seesaw with so much weight that price becomes almost irrelevant.

This means stacking your offer with bonuses, rewards, and money-back guarantees, which make it a no-brainer for your dream customer to say yes.

When you get this value/price equation right, selling will feel more like serving. You'll be able to charge premium prices confidently, knowing you're delivering far more value than you're asking for in return.

The Irresistible Offer

The foundation of any successful sale is an offer that your dream customer simply can't refuse. An irresistible offer provides massive value, minimizes risk, and creates such a sense of urgency that the sale becomes a foregone conclusion.

How do we craft an irresistible offer? It starts by doing something I like to call "value stacking." Value stacking means not just selling your core product or service but also stacking additional bonuses, exclusive content, personalized support, or anything else that enhances the perceived value of your offer.

The next thing you need to do to make an offer irresistible is to reduce the customer's risk as much as possible. Your prospect should feel like they have little to lose and everything to gain by saying yes to your offer. This could mean offering a solid money-back guarantee, a free trial period, or a reasonable payment plan.

Finally, you want to create a sense of urgency. This could be from communicating a limited-time discount, a few slots available, or any other element that encourages your prospect to act now rather than later.

The combination of massive value, little to no risk, and urgency to buy makes your customer feel like your product or service is the perfect solution for their problem and gets you the sale every time.

For example, when I decided to come out of retirement and build a $1M business in 12 months, I asked a group of entrepreneurs if they wanted to join me. The big promise was that I would let them tag along to watch over my shoulder so they could learn from someone who had done it multiple times before. But then, I also provided additional bonuses through weekly training, practical systems, weekly guidance, and a community of like-minded entrepreneurs who would support them. I also reduced their risk to almost zero by promising them that if they completed the course, I would refund their money as a reward.

I couldn't sell that program fast enough. It was so irresistible that I had to limit the number of people who could join because the response was overwhelming. Though unintentional, this limit created even more urgency for people to join.

The Lead Magnet

Even though your initial dream customers show great interest in your product and service when you validate it, it doesn't guarantee that future customers will buy.

This is especially true if building trust is important for your future dream customers to even consider buying.

The answer to building trust quickly with your dream customers is to offer them a lead magnet. In the same way, you wouldn't agree to marry someone on a first date, many customers first need to take small steps towards building trust with you before they consider buying.

A lead magnet is a free or low-cost offer that provides value upfront and helps to build enough trust with the customer to take the relationship to the next level. Therefore, the goal of a lead magnet is to convert a casual browser into a lead by offering them something of value in exchange for their contact information, creating the start of your relationship.

Some examples of effective lead magnets include:

1. eBooks or whitepapers
2. Checklists or cheat sheets
3. Video series or webinar training
4. Free trials or samples
5. Quizzes or self-assessments

To create a high-converting lead magnet, focus on providing highly valuable and actionable content that can provide quick, easy wins for your dream customer. Your lead magnet should be hyper-specific, easily consumable, and give a tangible result or transformation.

For example, one of my favorite lead magnets is giving away one of my books for free. My books are chock full of great value, so I will let customers download one for free in exchange for their contact information.

Another lead magnet I like to use is to tell customers they can try my Mobile App for free in exchange for their contact information. The app usually is free for everyone, but they don't need to know that. I lead them to the landing page first, get their email, and then send them to the app store to download the app for free.

The Value Ladder

Once you have your dream customer's information and you begin to nurture a relationship with them through social media or email content—the next step is to ask them to take the relationship to the next level with a purchase.

A value ladder, an idea made famous by Russell Brunson of ClickFunnels fame, is a sequence of offers to purchase. You price each purchase higher than the last, so the customer ascends, like climbing a ladder.

A value ladder aims to maximize customers' lifetime value by providing increasingly valuable solutions they can purchase over time.

A typical value ladder might look something like this:

1. Lead magnet (free or low-cost)
2. Quick offer ($7-$97)
3. Core offer ($997-$1997)
4. Premium offer ($4,997-$9,997)
5. High-ticket offer ($19,997+)

The key to an effective value ladder is ensuring each offer provides your customer with a logical next step and clear value progression. As they ascend the ladder, they should feel like they're getting more value at each level.

An example of a value ladder is the entrepreneur mastermind I mentioned previously. You may wonder how I made money since I refunded everyone at the end of the training. Well, I just gave them another irresistible offer at the end of the training that they could not refuse. I told them I would continue training them for a higher price for the next six months. And I told them they could roll over the money I was going to refund them, to cover the first month of this new program.

In their eyes, they got a free month on the new program, and I secured recurring revenue for the next six months. Win, win.

Therefore, adding a value ladder substantially increases the value of your customer, rather than settling for just one sale.

Irresistible Copywriting

Copywriting is the art and science of using words to persuade someone to take a desired action. When crafting irresistible offers, copywriting brings your offer to life and communicates its value to your dream customer.

Many entrepreneurs create a valuable solution, but because they cannot communicate the value, it falls on deaf ears.

Copywriting starts with understanding how humans think and communicating in a way aligned with their thought processes.

So, what are the key elements to tapping into your dream customer's deepest needs in a way that they can fully understand and get excited about?

Here are the five most essential elements to writing copy that converts:

1. Hook—Create attention-grabbing headlines.
What would catch your attention? A light tapping on the window, or a neighbor banging on your door telling you your house is on fire.

In such a noisy world, you must add elements to your writing that grab people's attention. Without attention, you will have no audience.

Extreme ideas, imagery, contradictions, and out-of-the-ordinary statements naturally grab attention and should be added to your copy.

2. Problem/Solution—Discuss your customer's problem and then make a big promise to solve it.

Your customer only cares about one thing: their problem. Therefore, when you talk about their problem, the customer will begin to believe you understand their situation well and trust that you can solve it.

Then, you can create more value by making a solid promise to solve the customer's problem and showing them how your product and service will solve it. Doing this will make your customers even more convinced and highly motivated to buy what you offer.

3. Payoff—Give them a vision of a better future.

Paint a clear and vivid picture of the transformation (payoff) your offer will provide and use language that resonates with your dream customer's deepest desires.

Help them imagine all the benefits and rewards they will experience after resolving their problem.

4. Story—Use vivid storytelling and imagery.

Suppose you wrap your information in a story. In that case, it will have a hypnotic effect on your customers, leading them to give you their undivided and open-minded attention.

It will also help melt away any internal resistance because stories can penetrate your customer's subconscious, helping to persuade them even more.

5. Proof—Use social proof and credibility markers (testimonials and reviews.)

One of the best ways to reduce customers' risk is to show them proof through testimonials and reviews from others. The more a customer sees that you have been able to deliver on your promise to others, the more certain they will be that you can do it for them.

6. CTA—Give a strong call-to-action.

Finally, a strong, commanding call to action will give your customer the direction and courage to take the next step. People are generally indecisive, but telling them what to do clarifies their next step and motivates them to act.

I realized how powerful these elements are the day I changed the way I presented my 30-second elevator pitch. In the past, people would ask me what I did, and I would share about my product or service and how it would benefit customers. Then, they would walk away.

Realizing that people are consumed by their problems, I decided to start my elevator pitch with the problem. "You know how entrepreneurs desire to make $1M, but they feel stuck not knowing what to do, or not being able to consistently execute? Well, I provide them with expert training and a supportive community to help them reach their first $1M in less than 18 months."

Now, instead of walking away, their immediate response would be, "Tell me more."

Upgrading Your Copywriting

One way to upgrade your copywriting is by formatting your copy using tested formulas proven to produce conversions. Some of these formulas are:

1. AIDA—Attention, Interest, Desire, Action
2. PAS—Problem, Agitate, Solution
3. BAB—Before, After, Bridge
4. 4 Ps—Picture, Promise, Prove, Push
5. FAB—Features, Advantages, Benefits
6. PASTOR—Problem, Agitate, Solution, Testimonials, Offer, Response
7. QUEST—Qualify, Understand, Educate, Stimulate, Transition

You can test which copy format works best for your dream customers. Yet, the key is always to cover all the previous six essential elements of copywriting.

The Core Story

Since you have been studying your dream customer for weeks, you ideally will already know their dreams, goals, desires, and pain points. This knowledge becomes a great asset that you can use in all your marketing and sales. It ultimately becomes the "Core Story" for all your sales assets.

A "Core Story" is an idea popularized by Chet Holmes in his book The Ultimate Sales Machine. It's a collection of all the valuable market research you have done for your dream customer, combined with authoritative information, woven into a compelling story that inspires your prospect to buy. It is a persuasive story that educates your prospect and creates a burning desire for your offer.

Remember, the goal in sales is to tap into your dream customer's desires and help them feel the severity of their problem. You also need to share new, compelling information that shifts your prospect's perspective and makes them eager to take action.

Your core story aims to do this by sharing shocking, compelling, and authoritative information, usually from statistics, data, and case studies, so your dream customer feels compelled to act.

Crafting Your Core Story

Here is a step-by-step process to craft your core story:

1. Identify the key problem your offer solves.
A deep understanding of the problem builds excellent rapport with your dream customer. It increases their faith in your ability to help them solve it.

2. Share shocking statistics or insights that highlight the severity of the problem.
This is where the true power of the core story comes in. When you can provide authoritative, proven statistical information that communicates the severity of your dream customer's problem in a shocking way, it quickly builds your customer's urgency to act. You can also provide information about the future consequences of not acting, which will significantly increase your prospect's urgency.

3. Introduce your unique solution and how it addresses the problem.
Here, you can also use statistics to show the most effective solutions to customers' problems. As you communicate the solution, you lean toward describing your own solution, which you will ultimately reveal as the obvious choice at the end of the core story.

4. Highlight the key benefits and outcomes of your solution.
Sharing how the solution is a perfect fit for the customer's problem also builds trust in the solution. This is especially true if the solution also perfectly fits their buying criteria.

5. Share proof, such as case studies or testimonials.
Here, you can use statistics to show the number of people who have solved the problem using the solution. Testimonials and reviews can support the credibility of the solution as well.

6. Address common objections and concerns.
You want to give your customer time to process this information and ask any questions. People will generally value the questions they ask more than what they are freely given. So answer all their questions and ask if they have any more.

7. End with a strong call-to-action.
Last, recap everything discussed, repeat the pain of the problem and the power of the solution, then introduce your product or service as the obvious choice for their situation. Then, give them a strong call to action to motivate them to act.

Following this structure, you create a compelling narrative that engages your prospect emotionally and intellectually and positions your offer as the clear choice to solve their problem.

You can also deliver a core story in person as a presentation, content, or a video sales letter that converts.

This core story framework greatly improved my cold-calling effectiveness and made it a joy. Instead of cold-calling prospects to try to get something from them, I would cold-call and offer them a great informative workshop that would benefit them. Then, I would present the core story and create so much value that I would easily move them to the next level of the sale.

The Irresistible Sales Process

Ideally, your copy, lead magnet, and core story will convince your prospect to attend a one-on-one sales meeting. At the meeting, you can use your sales process to close your prospects and inspire them to buy.

A systematic sales process is key to consistently converting prospects into paying customers. An irresistible sales process feels natural, conversational, and focused on serving the customer's needs, leading your prospect to ultimately say yes.

Here's a step-by-step breakdown of an effective sales process:

1. Qualify the prospect to ensure they're a good fit for your offer. If you do this right, this will do 90% of the heavy lifting even before the sales meeting.
2. Build rapport and trust through genuine conversation and active listening.
3. Identify the prospect's fundamental problems, goals, and desired future outcomes.

4. Share your solution as the obvious choice, showing how it perfectly meets their needs and buying criteria.
5. Address objections and concerns and answer any questions with empathy and clarity.
6. Provide a clear call-to-action, ask for the sale, and make it easy for the prospect to say yes.
7. Follow up consistently to nurture the relationship and provide ongoing value.

By following this process, you can guide your prospect from initial interest to excited customer, all while maintaining a spirit of service and authenticity.

Conclusion: Mastering the Art of Selling

Crafting irresistible offers and mastering the art of selling are essential skills for any entrepreneur looking to scale their business to $1M and beyond. By focusing on providing massive value, minimizing risk, and creating urgency, you can make offers your dream customers will find impossible to refuse.

Combine this with a compelling lead magnet, a value-packed ascension ladder, persuasive copywriting, a powerful core story, and a systematic sales process, and you'll have all the pieces in place to effortlessly enroll new customers.

Remember, at its core, selling is about serving. It's about deeply understanding your customers' needs and desires and offering a solution to transform their lives or businesses. When you approach sales from this perspective, it stops feeling icky or uncomfortable and starts feeling like a natural extension of the value you're already providing.

So go out there and craft your irresistible offers. Master the art of communicating value and guiding your prospects to a buying decision. Above all, focus on serving your dream customer at the highest level possible. With this approach, your first $1M is closer than you think.

ACTION STEPS

1. Write an irresistible offer that makes a big promise, stacks a lot of value, reduces the risk, and inspires urgency with your prospect.

2. Create a lead magnet that will inspire your customers to want to give you their contact information. Find a contractor on Upwork or Fiverr to build a landing page to offer your lead magnet and collect emails.

3. Use the copywriting skills in this chapter to present your irresistible offer and lead magnet in a compelling way, then go test it out in the marketplace.

If you want more proven systems to help you make your first million faster, join the 100X Entrepreneur's Club for FREE today: **100xClub.ai**.

Chapter 10

FUNDING AND BUILDING YOUR MILLION-DOLLAR IDEA

You've validated your solution, crafted an irresistible offer, and started generating sales. Congratulations! You're well on your way to building a thriving business.

But now comes the next challenge: actually creating and delivering your product or service at scale.

I still remember the first time I came up with my first great business idea. I thought it was the greatest thing since sliced bread. And I knew it would change the world.

But then the most life-sucking, dream-killing, soul-destroying thought came to my mind.

"How am I going to build this thing?"

Then, as quickly as my idea came, all my dreams went out the window and down the drain.

This was the pattern I would follow for many years to come. I would get a great idea, then quickly get discouraged because I didn't know how to put it together or how to get the money to build it.

And not surprisingly, a few months later, I would see someone make millions of dollars off my same idea.

Can you relate?

They say the greatest killer of an entrepreneur's dreams is the word "How."

The word "How?" doomed me to a life of entrepreneurial impotence, never being able to take my idea to market.

That is until I heard a phrase from Sir Richard Branson that changed my thinking forever.

The phrase?

"Just say yes and figure it out later."

Think Now, Not How

For many entrepreneurs, this is where the real fear and uncertainty sets in. How are you going to find the money to build your solution? How do you even create it, especially if you lack technical skills?

What if you can't deliver on your promises and disappoint your customers?

These are all valid concerns, but here's the good news: if you have a solution that people desperately want, finding the resources to build it becomes infinitely easier.

In this chapter, we'll explore some practical strategies for funding and building your million-dollar idea, even if you're starting from scratch.

Keep it Super Simple

When building your product or service, it's important to remember that your dream customers are primarily interested in the outcome—solving their problems. They don't necessarily care about all the bells and whistles or how polished everything looks right out of the gate.

As entrepreneurs, we often get caught up in trying to create the perfect product before launching. However, as Reid Hoffman, the founder of LinkedIn, famously said, "If you're not embarrassed by the first version of your product, you've launched too late."

The truth is that your customers mostly care about the core feature or benefit that directly addresses their pain points. They're not expecting a comprehensive, feature-rich solution right from the start.

In fact, trying to build too much too soon can actually slow you down and make it harder to get to market quickly.

There's also the issue of funding. Entrepreneurs often worry about how they will raise the money to develop their products, especially if they lack startup capital or investor backing.

Lastly, many entrepreneurs feel stuck when it comes to actually building out their product or service. They may lack the technical skills or knowledge to create their solution themselves or feel unsure how to find the right people to help them.

These concerns can lead to a lot of stress and anxiety, especially if you've already promised your solution to customers and feel pressure to deliver. You might worry that you won't be able to follow through and that you'll end up disappointing people or looking foolish.

To help you overcome these challenges, a helpful truth to remember is that finding money and people to help you build your product is never the real issue.

The real issue is finding a product or service that people desperately want in the first place.

Think of it like this: if you have a hot new product that thousands of people are clamoring for, you'll have no trouble finding the resources to produce and sell it. Manufacturers will be lining up to partner with you, investors will be eager to fund your growth, and customers will be beating down your door to buy.

On the other hand, if you have a product that nobody wants or needs, it won't matter how much money you have or how talented your team is.

The key, then, is to focus first and foremost on validating demand and creating a solution that genuinely resonates with your target market. Once you've done that, the rest becomes much easier. As the saying goes, "If you have a product or service that people desperately want, then you don't have any problems."

So don't let the challenges of funding and building your product hold you back. Stay focused on solving real problems for real people, and trust that the resources and support you need will follow.

With a little creativity and a lot of hustle, you can bring your million-dollar idea to life—and create something that your customers will truly love.

Here are some ideas on how to do just that.

Building a Minimum Viable Product (MVP)

One of the entrepreneurs' biggest mistakes is trying to build the perfect product or service right out of the gate. They spend months or even years developing a comprehensive solution with all the bells and whistles, only to find that the market doesn't want or need all those extra features.

The smarter approach is to start with a Minimum Viable Product (MVP) [or Minimum Viable Service (MVS)]—the simplest version of your solution that still solves your customer's core problem. By focusing on just one key feature or benefit, you can quickly and inexpensively bring your MVP to market and start gathering honest feedback from paying customers.

The specifics of your MVP will depend on your business model and industry. For example:

- If you're in e-commerce or print-on-demand, your MVP might be a small initial batch of products or basic designs.
- If you're creating an online course or coaching program, your MVP could be a simple outline or curriculum that you deliver live to a small group of beta students.
- If you're building a software product, your MVP might be a basic app with just one core feature rather than a full suite of tools.

The key is to resist the temptation to over-build or over-complicate things right from the start. Keep your MVP lean, focused, and centered around solving your customer's most pressing problem. You can always add more features and complexity later once you've validated that your core solution resonates with your market.

For example, when we first introduced our birdwatching binoculars to the market, the truth was that they weren't very pretty. The optics were incredible, but the aesthetics weren't anything to write home for. Yet, we still sold tens of thousands of them. Why? because the customers only cared about one thing: the amazing experience they had watching birds.

After a few months, we decided to introduce more sleek designs and other features, but even then, customers were not as impressed with the design as they were with the optics.

Creative Funding Strategies

Of course, even building an MVP requires some level of investment, whether that's in time, money, or both. But here's the thing: you don't necessarily need a ton of startup capital or venture funding to get your idea off the ground. In fact, relying too heavily on outside investment can often be a recipe for losing control of your vision and direction.

Instead, consider some of these creative funding strategies to bootstrap your way to success:

1. Presales and deposits

Offer special discounts or bonuses to customers willing to pay or put a deposit upfront for your product or service before it's fully developed. This can give you the cash flow you need to fund production without taking on debt.

2. Let your customers fund your business

By charging premium prices and upselling your customers, you can set up your business so that your customers pay for everything. For example, imagine if the money you make from your customers is 3X-5X the amount it costs to acquire them and fulfill your promise. This means that the customers not only pay for themselves, but now you have money left over to acquire more customers and have a healthy profit.

As long as you keep getting and upselling new customers, you will never have to worry about money to grow your business.

3. Crowdfunding

If you've already validated demand for your product, why not let your customers fund its development? Platforms like Kickstarter and Indiegogo allow you to prefund your product and raise the capital you need to bring it to life.

4. Partnerships and revenue-sharing

Look for strategic partners who have resources or skills that complement your own. For example, you might partner with a manufacturer willing to produce your product in exchange for a percentage of future sales.

5. Freelancing and consulting

If you have marketable skills or expertise, consider working freelance or consulting to generate extra income to invest in your business. This can be a great way to fund your venture while maintaining full control.

6. Start a side business

Use the other business model ideas in this book to make extra money to funnel into your new venture.

The key is to get creative and think outside the box when it comes to funding your venture. Don't let a lack of capital keep you from pursuing your vision. Where there is a resourceful and creative will, there's always a way.

For example, one of my students used Kickstarter and Indiegogo to validate his business and fund the production and shipping of his physical product. There was such a huge demand for his product that he ended up making $1M in less than four months. Now, crowdfunding is his go-to strategy for validating and funding all his ventures.

 Reflection Exercise

1. What funding sources can you tap into that you have not considered?
2. What ideas on this list seem feasible for you to tap into now and raise your funding?

Building an All-Star Team

To build your product or service, you'll likely reach a point where you realize you need more expertise to take it to the next level. You'll need to build a team of skilled professionals to help you get your product or service consumer-ready. But how do you find the right people, especially working with a limited budget?

One approach is to focus on finding partners or collaborators rather than just employees. Look for people who share your vision and values and have complementary skills or resources to help you achieve your goals faster. For example:

- If you're a marketer with a great product idea, look for a technical co-founder to help you build it.
- If you're an artist or creative, partner with a business-savvy entrepreneur who can help you monetize your talents.

- If you have a brick-and-mortar business, contact an online marketer who can help you expand your reach and customer base.

Another option is to leverage online platforms and marketplaces to find talented freelancers and contractors worldwide. Sites like Upwork and Fiverr make finding skilled professionals in design, development, and marketing easier, often at a fraction of the cost of hiring full-time employees.

The key is building a lean, agile team to help you execute your vision without breaking the bank. Look for people who are passionate about your mission, have a track record of delivering results, and are willing to roll up their sleeves and do whatever it takes to help your business succeed.

Conclusion: People, Partners, and Resources

Building and funding your million-dollar idea can be a big challenge, especially starting from scratch. But with the right strategies and mindset, it's achievable.

Remember, your job as an entrepreneur is not to have all the answers or to do everything yourself. It's to be resourceful, creative, and persistent in finding the people, partners, and resources you need to bring your vision to life.

Start by creating a lean, inexpensive, focused MVP that solves your customer's core problem. Validate demand and generate revenue as quickly as possible, even if your solution isn't perfect right out of the gate.

From there, get creative with your funding strategies. Look for ways to bootstrap, presell, and partner your way to profitability without relying too heavily on outside investment or debt.

As you grow, build a team of passionate, skilled professionals who share your vision and can help you take your business to the next level. Focus on finding the right partners and collaborators and leverage online platforms and marketplaces to access top talent from around the world.

Above all, don't let a lack of resources or expertise keep you from pursuing your dreams. As I said previously, "If you have a product or service that people desperately want, then you don't have any problems." Focus on solving real problems for real people and trust that the rest will fall into place.

With hustle, heart, and a little creative problem-solving, you can fund and build your way to a million-dollar business—and beyond. So what are you waiting for? It's time to roll up your sleeves and get to work.

ACTION STEPS

1. Start building your MVP or MVS with only the main feature that solves your dream customers' pain points.

2. List all the creative funding ideas you will use and start raising money.

3. Go on contractor sites like Fiverr or Upwork to find the professionals to help you build your MVP or MVS.

If you want more proven systems to help you make your first million faster, join the 100X Entrepreneur's Club for FREE today: **100xClub.ai**.

Chapter 11

MAXIMIZING CUSTOMER VALUE

Congratulations! You've successfully launched your product or service and started acquiring customers. But the journey doesn't end there. It's just the beginning of a long-term partnership that, if nurtured properly, can lead to exponential growth and success for your business.

In this chapter, we'll explore the art and science of managing customers and maximizing their lifetime value. We'll explore why customers are the lifeblood of your business and how you can partner with them to meet their evolving needs and unlock multiple levels of value.

Why Customer Relationships Matter

When I first entered entrepreneurship, I thought a relationship with a customer was one-and-done. They bought it once, and then that was the end of our relationship.

It finally dawned on me that I was missing out on something great when someone described a relationship with your customer like a marriage. I mean, can you imagine getting married and then never seeing your spouse again?

I heard Russell Brunson describe customers this way when he taught about sales funnels. He explained that the goal of acquiring a customer is to build long-lasting and fulfilling relationships with them. This also meant identifying more of their needs and selling them more and more products over time. The idea was that by doing this, the customers would reciprocate by abundantly rewarding me with more and more profit for years to come.

This is when I finally understood the secret of the long-term value of a customer.

The Problem with One-and-Done Thinking

Without customers, you have no business. It's as simple as that. Your customers are the ones who provide the revenue and feedback that fuel your growth and success.

But beyond just being a source of income, your customers are also your greatest asset regarding revenue growth, marketing, innovation, and competitive advantage. By building strong, long-lasting relationships with your customers, you can tap into a goldmine of insights, ideas, and opportunities that can take your business to the next level.

Too often, though, entrepreneurs focus all their energy on acquiring new customers while neglecting the ones they already have. They see each sale as a one-time transaction rather than the start of a long-term partnership.

This approach leaves a lot of value on the table. It's far more expensive to acquire a new customer than to retain an existing one.

Also, repeat customers spend more, refer more, and provide more valuable feedback than new ones.

Plus, if you're not actively working to meet your customers' needs and exceed their expectations, you risk losing them to competitors who are. In today's hyper-competitive market, customer loyalty is no longer a given—it's something you must earn and re-earn every day.

The 100X Customer Value Cycle

So, how do you build lasting relationships with your customers that lead to ever-growing revenue and profits? The key is to follow what I call the 100X Customer Value Cycle—a systematic approach to maximizing customer lifetime value (CLV) through ongoing engagement, support, and feedback.

Here's how it works:

1. Initial Purchase

Start by providing an exceptional buying experience that sets the stage for a long-term relationship. Ensure your onboarding process is smooth, your product or service delivers on its promises, and your customer feels valued and appreciated.

2. Upsell and Cross-Sell

Look for opportunities to offer new products or services to your customers, providing additional value. The key is to focus on their needs and desires rather than just trying to increase sales.

3. Ask for Referrals

Happy customers are your best marketers. Encourage them to refer their friends and colleagues to your business and make it easy for them to do so through referral programs, incentives, or simple sharing tools.

4. Gather Social Proof

Ask your satisfied customers to provide testimonials, reviews, or case studies for your marketing materials. This social proof can help build trust and credibility with new prospects and make it easier to close more sales.

5. Seek Feedback

Regularly check in with your customers to gather feedback on their experience with your product or service. Use this feedback to identify areas for improvement and show your customers that you value their input and are committed to meeting their needs.

6. Provide Ongoing Support

Ensure your customers have easy access to helpful resources, tutorials, and support whenever needed. This could include a knowledge base, video guides, live chat, or phone support—whatever makes sense for your business and customers' preferences.

7. Nurture the Relationship

Stay in touch with your customers through regular communication, such as email newsletters, social media updates, or personalized check-ins. The goal is to provide ongoing value and build a sense of community and connection.

8. Innovate and Improve

Use the insights and feedback you gather from your customers to continuously improve your offerings and develop new products or services that meet their evolving needs. The more you can anticipate and solve your customers' problems, the more valuable you become to them.

By consistently following this cycle, you can turn one-time buyers into lifelong fans and advocates and maximize the value of each customer relationship over time.

For example, one thing that I try to do is get with a few of my dream customers every month. Though it takes time and effort, it pays off in customer loyalty and valuable customer insights. I can stay on top of my customers' needs, find out where they are unsatisfied, and then produce new products and services I can sell them. By being close to my customers in this way, I increase the value of our company exponentially.

Reflection Exercise

1. What are some things on this list you can start doing to help your customers feel more valued and connected?

2. How can you set up a routine to do these things systematically for each customer?

The Power of Community

One of the most powerful ways to strengthen customer relationships is to foster a sense of community around your brand. When customers feel like they're part of something bigger than just a transaction, they're more likely to stick around, spend more, and tell others about your business.

There are many ways to build a community, depending on your industry and target market. Here are a few ideas:

- Create a private Facebook group, WhatsApp chat, or online forum where customers can connect with each other and with your team.
- Host live events, webinars, or meetups that bring your customers together around a shared interest or goal.
- Feature user-generated content on your website or social media channels, and celebrate your customers' successes and milestones.
- Offer exclusive perks, discounts, or experiences to your most loyal customers and make them feel like VIPs.

The key is to create opportunities for your customers to interact with each other and your brand in meaningful ways and to make them feel like they're part of something special.

My favorite tool for this is WhatsApp. Our WhatsApp group is buzzing daily with new insights, resources, comments, and victories that my dream customers share with one another. I try to be active on the chat, but even when I am not, others actively engage with the community, making it a vibrant and fulfilling experience.

The Art of the Follow-Up

Another crucial aspect of customer management is mastering the follow-up. This means proactively contacting your customers after the sale to check in on their experience, gather feedback, and look for opportunities to provide additional value.

The exact schedule and format of your follow-up will depend on your business model and customer preferences, but here are some general guidelines to consider:

- Send a personalized thank-you message immediately after the purchase, and include any necessary onboarding information or resources.
- Check-in after a week or two to make sure your customer is satisfied with their purchase and to answer any questions they may have.
- Send regular updates or newsletters with helpful tips, industry news, or exclusive offers.

- Reach out periodically to gather feedback on specific aspects of your product or service and use that feedback to make improvements.
- Celebrate your customers' milestones or achievements, and show them that you're invested in their success.

By staying in touch with your customers and showing them that you care about their experience, you can build trust and loyalty that will pay dividends for your business over time.

Conclusion: Customers, Your Greatest Asset

Managing customers and maximizing their lifetime value is not a one-time event but an ongoing process that requires consistent effort and attention. By following the 100X Customer Value Cycle, building community, and mastering the art of follow-up, you can turn your customers into your greatest asset and unlock exponential growth for your business.

But it all starts with a mindset shift—from seeing customers as transactions to seeing them as partners in your success. When you genuinely care about your dream customers' needs, desires, and success, and are willing to go above and beyond to help them achieve their goals, you'll find that they'll become your biggest advocates and allies.

So start by reaching out to your existing customers today. Ask them how they're doing, what you can do to support them, and what feedback or ideas they have for improving your offerings. Listen carefully to their responses and use them to guide your customer management strategy.

Remember, your customers are the lifeblood of your business. By treating them like the valuable partners they are and consistently working to meet their needs and exceed their expectations, you'll be well on your way to building a thriving, sustainable business that makes a real difference in people's lives.

And that's what entrepreneurship is all about—not just making money but positively impacting the world and the people you serve. So go out there and start building those relationships, one customer at a time. Your million-dollar business (and your customers) will thank you for it.

ACTION STEPS

1. **Speak to 5-10 of your dream customers and:**

   - Find out how they are doing, and if there is any-thing you can do for them.

   - Ask for feedback.

   - Ask for referrals.

If you want more proven systems to help you make your first million faster, join the 100X Entrepreneur's Club for FREE today: **100xClub.ai**.

Chapter 12

HOW TO MANAGE EVERYTHING AND STAY SANE

You might find this hard to believe, but I am lazy.

I am so lazy that if I work more than 3 hours a day, I feel an overwhelming sense that something is wrong with the world.

I used to feel bad about my laziness until I read a quote by Robert Heinlein that went like this:

"Progress isn't made by early risers, but by lazy people trying to find easier ways to do things."

That's when I realized that my laziness was my superpower. Why? Because it forced me to look for easier, faster, and more effective ways to get 10X results while using 10X less time, effort, resources, and money.

It taught me the power of 100X.

Managing the Flood

Entrepreneurship can feel like trying to build a dam while the floodgates are open. A million tasks demand your attention, from marketing and sales to managing customers, delivering value, and keeping the finances in order.

It's easy to feel overwhelmed like you're drowning in a sea of to-dos.

You may be working 12-hour days and still feel like you're not getting enough done. You're constantly switching between tasks, feeling like you have entrepreneurial ADHD. The passion and excitement you once felt for your business have been replaced by stress and exhaustion.

But here's the good news: if you're busy as an entrepreneur, it means people want what you're offering. The demand is there, and that's half the battle.

The key now is learning how to manage the flood of tasks and responsibilities in a way that allows you to stay focused, productive, and sane.

The Paradox of Productivity

The solution lies in a concept I call the Paradox of Productivity. It states:

1. If you have to do more, focus on less.
2. If you want to go faster, move slower.
3. If you want to be greater, go deeper.

In other words, the key to accomplishing more isn't to try to do everything at once. It's to focus on the most important things, to give them your full attention, and to do them exceptionally well.

This brings us back to two core principles we've discussed before:

1. The 80/20 Principle
80% of your results come from 20% of your efforts. Focus on identifying and prioritizing that crucial 20%.

2. EADS
For the remaining 80% of tasks, you can Eliminate, Automate, Delegate, or Simplify.

The Problem with Perpetual Motion

The challenge is, how do you put these principles into practice when you're in the whirlwind of entrepreneurship? How do you identify which tasks are essential and which ones can be EADS'ed? How do you find the time to step back and organize your work when you're already working around the clock?

It can feel like you're on a hamster wheel, running faster and faster but not getting anywhere. You're in a state of perpetual motion but not necessarily making progress.

As Abraham Lincoln famously said, "Give me six hours to chop down a tree, and I will spend the first four sharpening the axe." The point is that taking the time to strategize and plan your work is just as important as the actual execution, if not more so.

The 100X Ultimate Time Management Process

That's where the 100X Ultimate Time Management Process comes in. It's a simple but powerful framework for managing your time and tasks as an entrepreneur. It consists of three key steps:

1. Focus: Identify and focus on what's most valuable.
2. Review: Review progress and look for ways to improve.
3. Execute: Execute the new plan through routines and systems.

Let's break each of these down:

Step 1: Focus on What's Most Important

In the whirlwind of entrepreneurship, it's easy to lose sight of what really matters. Urgent tasks have a way of crowding out important ones. So, the first step is to regain that clarity and focus.

How do you know if something is truly valuable? Simple: it brings money or other forms of capital into your business. This could be sales, revenue, profit, equity, influence, opportunities, or anything else that contributes to the growth and success of your venture.

Here are a few examples of the highest-value tasks in most businesses:

- Getting to know your customers' and partners' greatest needs.
- Making offers and closing sales.
- Reaching out to potential Dream 100 customers or influencers.
- Joining and interacting with high-powered groups or masterminds.
- Setting up appointments with influential people.
- Researching trends and niches for new business ideas.
- Finding and recruiting top talent for your team.
- Leveraging money to generate higher ROI.
- Streamlining and optimizing your time through EADS.
- Planning, strategizing, and improving systems.

In addition to your Highest-Value Tasks, look for what I call Exponential Triggers. These are opportunities or activities that have the potential for a 100X return because of their impact. Examples could be capitalizing on a hot trend, forming a key strategic partnership, or developing game-changing technology.

One big exponential trigger I value highly is capitalizing on a hot trend. I have accomplished more by tapping into a hot trend in a year than I have by pouring out my own blood, sweat, and tears in a decade. This is the power of exponential triggers, which can provide 10X-100X returns in a very short period.

Step 2: Review and Improve

The second step is regularly reviewing your progress and looking for ways to improve. As Peter Drucker said, "Whatever you measure improves."

I recommend conducting a weekly and monthly review using the following process:

The Big W's

- WWW: What Went Well?
- WDW: What Didn't Go Well?
- WDL: What Did You Learn?
- WDD: What Will You Do Differently?

Big Rock Goals Review

In addition, pick Big Rock Goals you want to accomplish each month, then review your progress. See how well you've achieved the milestones to help you reach your monthly Big Rock Goals every week.

20/80 Tasks Review

Next, look at how you did with your High-Value 20% activities, which bring 80% of the returns. How well did you focus on the 20%? Look at your schedule. What will you do to ensure you stay focused on the 20% this week? Celebrate your wins and look for ways to improve.

Exponential Triggers Review

Review any Exponential Triggers you were focusing on for the month. Did you make progress? Did new opportunities emerge?

Make Your New Plan

Based on your review, set your new Big Rock Goals, 20% Tasks, Exponential Triggers, and priorities for the coming week or month.

Then ask yourself, "What steps do I need to take to move the needle this next week/month?"

Step 3: Execute Through Routines

The last step is to translate your priorities into action through the power of routines. As the saying goes, "A good routine can overcome a weak character."

Routines are what ensure consistency in execution, and consistent execution is the foundation of all success.

One of my favorite routines is what I call "Roles and Flow":

- First, identify your key roles in your business and life. A role is anything you're responsible for the outcome of. This could be a specific business or project or a personal role like being a spouse or parent.
- Then, assign each role to a specific day of the week. For example, Mondays might be for your primary business, Tuesdays for a side project, Wednesdays for business development, etc.
- On the assigned day, block off 2 hours for uninterrupted "flow" time to make progress on that role's top priorities.

For example, here is what my typical week looks like:

- Monday: Bitcoin and investments.
- Tuesday: Book publishing business.
- Wednesday: Coaching and information products.
- Thursday: SaaS and mobile apps.
- Friday: "Moonshot" new business venture.
- Saturday: Break / personal time.
- Sunday: Planning and strategy.

Within each of these Focus Blocks, I spend 2 hours daily working on my top 20% activities for that role.

The power of this routine provides three significant benefits:

1. It ensures that your key responsibilities get focus time every week. Nothing slips through the cracks.
2. It allows for deep, focused work, which is when we're at our most productive and creative. 2 hours of uninterrupted flow is often more productive than a scattered full day of work.
3. It reduces multi-tasking and mental clutter. Knowing that each role has its time and place, you can be fully present with what's in front of you.

By applying the Roles and Flow routine I would spend two hours a day in flow time. Then I would use an hour to follow up on other important items for the week. Last, I might have a meeting with a high-value connection as well. In total, this routine is so effective, it reduced my workday to only 3-4 hours.

Other Tips and Accelerators

In addition to the core time management strategies I've discussed, here are some other productivity tips and techniques I've found useful:

- **Live Above the Line**—During your flow time, list the three most valuable tasks that need to be done and draw a line. Then, list everything else after. Focus on doing the big three above the line before anything else.
- **The 2-Minute Rule:** If a task takes less than 2 minutes, just do it now.
- **Pomodoro Technique:** Work in focused 25-minute sprints with 5-minute breaks in between.
- **"Eat That Frog":** Do your most important (and often most challenging) task before anything else.
- **Batching:** Group similar tasks together and do them in one go. For example, make all your calls or answer emails at a designated time.
- **Stop-Doing List:** Regularly review what you need to STOP doing to free up time and energy.
- **Prepare Tomorrow Today:** At the end of each day, plan out your tasks and priorities for the next day. This allows you to hit the ground running in the morning.
- **Use Technology:** Leverage tools for task management, scheduling, automation, and outsourcing. Let tech do the heavy lifting.
- **Say No:** Guard your time fiercely. Say no to anything that isn't a hell yes.
- **Single-tasking:** Multi-tasking is a myth. Focus on one thing at a time, and you'll do it better and faster.

- **Gap and Gain:** Focus on your progress (the gain), not the distance you still have to go (the gap). This will keep you motivated.

Conclusion: Success is a Marathon

Entrepreneurship is a marathon, not a sprint. To succeed in the long run, you need sustainable productivity and time management systems.

The 100X Ultimate Time Management Process of Focus, Review, and Execute gives you a simple but powerful framework from which to operate. You'll be amazed at how much you can accomplish in far less time by consistently focusing on your high-value 20% activities, reviewing and improving each week, and executing through the power of routines.

Remember, it's not about doing more; it's about focusing on what matters most. It's not about going faster but making consistent, meaningful progress. And it's not about being busy; it's about going deep on the things that truly move the needle.

So, take a step back from the whirlwind today. Sharpen your axe. Identify your 20% activities. Block off some Focus Time. And most of all, give yourself grace. Productivity is a practice, and every day is a new opportunity to optimize and improve.

You've got this. Now go focus on what matters, and let's 100X your productivity and performance.

ACTION STEPS

1. List all your business roles.

2. Assign each role to a specific day of the week.

3. Set up 2 hours of flow time for each role and test your roles and flow strategy this week.

If you want more proven systems to help you make your first million faster, join the 100X Entrepreneur's Club for FREE today: **100xClub.ai**.

Chapter 13

THE 100X ACCELERATORS: BUILDING AN ENTREPRENEURIAL WAR CHEST

Growing up, people have always told me that if I worked hard, I would be successful.

That is until I found myself working two jobs, attending school full-time, actively leading multiple groups at my church, and trying to keep my wife and kids happy.

When it was all said and done, I looked at my bank account, and it was empty, flashing bright red with a fat negative sign in front of it.

Then it dawned on me. "If I keep doing what everyone else is doing, I am going to get the ordinary results everyone else is getting."

So I started looking for extraordinary solutions, things no one was talking about, secrets only a few radical people were willing to try.

That's when I learned that there is an entire world full of what I call 100X Accelerators.

100X Accelerators are uncommon opportunities that, if tapped into, can provide you with an unimaginable level of returns that people only dream of. It's like the 80/20 principle on steroids.

The good news is that these 100X Accelerator opportunities are everywhere if you are willing to look for them. As a matter of fact, successful entrepreneurs make it a habit of collecting these opportunities, giving them their edge in business.

Now, I want to show you how to tap into these opportunities also.

Building An Arsenal of Assets

Have you ever felt like you're starting your entrepreneurial journey from scratch with no money, contacts, or resources? Maybe you've watched other entrepreneurs effortlessly build successful businesses and wondered, "How do they do it? What do they have that I don't?"

The truth is that successful entrepreneurs aren't just winging it. They're not starting from zero every time they launch a new venture. Instead, they've built a powerful arsenal of assets, relationships, and capabilities to leverage across any business they start.

These assets are the 100X Accelerators, which allow them to jumpstart any business easily and effortlessly, weather any storm, and seize opportunities that others can't.

Think of it as a country building up its military, even during peace-time. Would you rather face a potential conflict with no army and no resources or with a well-equipped, well-trained force ready to mobilize at a moment's notice?

The same principle applies in business. By continually cultivating these key accelerators, you'll be ready for anything—whether that's capitalizing on a sudden market opportunity, bouncing back from a setback, or scaling your business to new heights.

The 100X Accelerators

So, what are these critical assets every entrepreneur should be building? Here's my list of the top 100X Accelerators:

1. Network of High-Value Influencers
One of the most powerful assets you can have as an entrepreneur is a strong network of influential people. These people can open doors, make introductions, and lend credibility and resources to your ventures.

To build this network, prioritize regularly connecting with high-value individuals in your industry and beyond. But don't just focus on what they can do for you—look for ways to add value to them first. Offer your skills, connections, and insights. Build genuine relationships based on mutual benefit.

Action Step:
Set a goal to have a meaningful interaction with at least one influential person each week. This could be a coffee meeting,

a Zoom call, or even a thoughtful email exchange. Focus on serving them and providing value.

2. Partnerships

Another key accelerator is the power of partnerships. The right business partner can bring complementary skills, resources, and networks to the table, allowing you to achieve far more together than you could alone.

Look for partners who share your values and vision but bring a different set of strengths. Some common partnership structures include:

- Visionary + Operator
- Business Expert + Technical Expert
- Marketing/Sales + Operations

The key is to find someone who fills in your gaps and vice versa. When you leverage each other's strengths, you can 2X, 5X, or even 10X your impact and efficiency.

Action Step:

Identify the key areas where a partner could help you level up. Start putting feelers out there and having exploratory conversations with potential collaborators.

3. Mastermind Groups and Communities

Participating in high-level mastermind groups and entrepreneurial communities is like networking on steroids. Not only do you get to build relationships with a curated group of ambitious professionals, but you also get to tap into the collective wisdom and resources of the group.

The right mastermind can help you troubleshoot challenges, get fresh perspectives on opportunities, and make quantum leaps in your mindset and strategy. Many of my most significant breakthroughs have come from hot seats and impactful conversations within masterminds.

Action Step:

Research the top masterminds and communities in your industry or niche. Be willing to apply and invest in the groups that are the best fit. The ROI on these groups can be massive.

4. Social Capital and Goodwill

Your reputation and your relationships are everything in business. The more you focus on serving others and delivering value, the more social capital and goodwill you build.

This isn't about keeping score or expecting tit-for-tat favors. It's about being generous, trustworthy, and the kind of person others want to support and do business with. When you lead with value, opportunities and resources flow your way.

Action Step:

Look for opportunities each day to serve someone in your network without expecting anything in return. Share a resource, make an introduction, and offer feedback or advice. Make generosity your default mode.

5. Strong Personal Brand

A strong personal brand is a powerful asset in today's noisy marketplace. When you're known for something—an area of expertise, a unique methodology, a provocative viewpoint—people will seek you out for it.

Your personal brand helps you cut through the clutter and attract the right opportunities and clients. It allows you to charge a premium and be seen as a trusted authority.

To build your brand, define what you want to be known for. What are your unique strengths and points of view? Then, start creating content and conversations around those topics. Write articles, post on social media, speak on podcasts, and teach workshops. The more you put your ideas out there, the stronger your brand becomes.

Action Step:

Define your top 3-5 areas of expertise or unique viewpoints. Brainstorm a list of content ideas around each one. Commit to creating and sharing one piece of content daily to build your brand.

6. Engaged Audience and Superfans

One of the most valuable assets you can build is an engaged audience of fans and followers. These people know, like, and trust you—they will buy your products, share your content, and evangelize your brand.

Building an audience takes time and consistency, but it pays enormous dividends. With an audience, you have a built-in customer base for any new product or service. You have a direct line of communication to gather feedback and ideas. You have an army of supporters ready to spread the word.

To build your audience, focus on providing massive value. Share insights, tell stories, entertain, educate. Be consistent in showing up and interacting often with your community. Over time, you'll cultivate a loyal tribe supporting you in everything you do.

Action Step:

Choose one primary platform (e.g., email list, LinkedIn, Instagram, YouTube) to focus on building your audience. Commit to showing up there regularly with valuable content. Set a goal for your audience size six months from now and work backward to create a content plan.

7. Outsourcing and Technology

As an entrepreneur, your time and energy are your most precious resources. The more you can automate and outsource low-level tasks, the more you can focus on your zone of genius—the high-value, high-impact activities that truly move the needle.

Leveraging technology is critical to scaling your impact without burning yourself out. Tools like AI, automation software, social media scheduling, project management software, and virtual assistants can free up massive amounts of time and mental bandwidth.

Action Step:

Make a list of all the repetitive tasks you do each week. Research tools or services that could automate or streamline each one. Implement the top 1-2 solutions that save you the most time.

8. Access to Capital

While bootstrapping can be a great way to start, most fast-growing businesses need an infusion of capital to scale. Access to funding—whether through investors, loans, or grants—can be the difference between plateauing and exploding your growth.

Building relationships with investors and lenders before you need their money is key. The best time to look for funding is when you don't desperately need it. Focus on getting to know potential funders, understanding their investment criteria, and keeping them updated on your progress.

Action Step:

List 10-20 potential funding sources for your business. These could be individual investors, venture capital firms, banks, or grant programs. Research each one and identify the next step to start building a relationship, such as attending an event they host or asking for an introductory meeting.

9. Optimized Marketing System

A well-oiled marketing machine is like having a reliable stream of leads and sales on tap. When you've taken the time to build out your marketing funnels, your conversion mechanisms, and your customer acquisition systems, you can more easily scale your business and weather any market changes.

Focus on creating evergreen assets like a strong core story, a compelling website, a valuable lead magnet, an effective sales funnel, and an engaging email sequence. Test and optimize your messaging and your traffic sources. Build out your exponential marketing tactics while automating or delegating the incremental ones.

Action Step:

Map out your current customer journey from awareness to purchase to upsell. Identify any gaps or weak points in the process. Prioritize the top 1-2 improvements you can make to your marketing system this quarter. Focus most of your time on exponential marketing efforts.

10. Distribution Channels and Partnerships

Getting your product or service into the hands of more customers is the key to rapid growth. However, building your distribution channels from scratch can be slow and expensive. That's where leveraging other people's networks and platforms comes in.

Focus on building strategic distribution partnerships with individuals or companies that already have the attention and trust of your dream customers. This could involve creating an affiliate program for influencers or establishing a strategic partnership with other business owners who serve your target market but don't compete with you.

Action Step:

Brainstorm a list of 10-20 individuals or companies serving your dream customers. Rank them by potential impact. Contact the top names to discuss potential partnership opportunities.

11. Talent and Expert Network

As your business grows, you'll need to expand your team and expert support network. However, finding the right people can be time-consuming, and hiring the wrong fit can be costly. That's why it's important to always build your talent pipeline and list of expert contractors.

Make a habit of collecting resumes and work samples from promising candidates, even if you're not actively hiring. Build relationships with top freelancers and agencies so you have them on speed dial when a need arises. Having a bench of pre-vetted talent can save you countless hours and headaches when it's time to expand your team.

Action Step:

Create a spreadsheet to track potential hires and expert contractors. Include columns for name, contact info, area of expertise, and notes. Make a plan to add at least one new name each week, even if you're not actively hiring.

12. Continuous Improvement and Innovation

In today's fast-paced market, the businesses that thrive are the ones that are constantly evolving and innovating. What worked yesterday may not work tomorrow, so it's crucial to have a system for continuous improvement woven into your company culture.

Set aside time each week to review your key metrics and identify areas for improvement. Encourage your team to pitch new ideas and run small experiments. Stay on top of industry trends and look for ways to be an early adopter of new technologies or strategies.

Action Step:

Implement a weekly "10% meeting" with your team, where you identify one area of the business that needs improvement by 10% that week. Rotate who leads the meeting each week so everyone has a chance to contribute ideas.

13. Investing in Yourself (CANEI)

Finally, and perhaps most importantly, your business's greatest growth accelerator is your own personal growth. As your skills, knowledge, network, and mindset expand, so do your opportunities and your capacity to execute on them.

Commit to being a lifelong learner. Read books and articles from experts in your field. Attend workshops and conferences to sharpen your skills and make new connections. Invest in coaching or mentorship to help you break through to the next level. The more you grow, the more your business will grow.

Action Step:

List the top 3 skills or knowledge gaps you want to develop in the next six months—research courses, books, or mentors that can help you level up in each area. Block off dedicated learning time in your weekly calendar.

Conclusion: Compounding Your Growth Over Time

Building these 100X Accelerators is not a one-time event but an ongoing process. It's about consistently investing in the assets and capabilities that will compound your growth over time.

The key is to focus on adding value at every turn. With every inter-action, every piece of content, every new connection, ask yourself: "How can I make this as valuable as possible for the other person?" The more value you put into the world, the more it will come back to you in the form of opportunities, resources, and support.

Remember, your business can only grow as fast as you do. By continually improving yourself and building out these key accel-erators, you'll be ready to seize any opportunity and weather any challenge that comes your way.

Imagine how much easier and faster your entrepreneurial journey will be when you have a powerful network, a strong brand, an optimized system, and a war chest of resources at your fingertips. That's the power of the 100X Accelerators.

So start building them today. Don't wait until you need them to begin developing these assets. The earlier and more consistently you invest in them, the greater the payoff will be.

ACTION STEPS

1. Pick 1-2 Accelerators you can make improvements on this month.

2. Repeat it each month.

If you want more proven systems to help you make your first million faster, join the 100X Entrepreneur's Club for FREE today: **100xClub.ai**.

Conclusion

YOUR MILLION DOLLAR DESTINY AWAITS

We've covered a lot of ground on this journey, from zero to $1 million. From mastering your mindset to choosing your business model, from finding your dream customer to crafting your irresistible offer, funding your idea, and building your team, you now have a comprehensive roadmap for entrepreneurial success.

But this isn't just about tactics and strategies. It's about a fundamental shift in how you approach business and life. It's about adopting the mindset of a 100X entrepreneur who thinks bigger, acts bolder, and achieves more than most people dream possible.

Remember, your success starts with your psychology. Cultivate the 7 Core Mindsets of successful entrepreneurs and commit to the 10 Commitments that create unstoppable momentum. Condition yourself for success through the 4-step process of Transformation, Visualization, Saturation, and Implementation.

Internalize the 18 Commandments of Entrepreneurial Success. These are your guiding principles, north star, and cheat codes for the game of business. They'll keep you on track when things get tough and help you make the right decisions under pressure.

Choose your entrepreneurial vehicle wisely. Whether it's e-commerce, software, coaching, or any other top business models we covered, find the one that aligns with your strengths and passions. Then, use accelerators to hit the gas and reach your goals faster.

Become obsessed with serving your dream customer. Fall in love with their problems, desires, and dreams. Craft a solution so valuable and irresistible that they can't help but buy. Then, overdeliver on your promises and create customers for life.

When crafting your ideal solution, aim to become an indispensable partner in your customers' lives. Obsess over understanding their deepest needs, desires, and challenges, and relentlessly innovate to solve their problems better than anyone else. Use the 100X Solution Creation Criteria as your guide: create an offer that effectively solves your dream customer's problem, is easy and enjoyable to use, delivers a delightful experience, is profitable for you, and can scale to the masses.

Validation is the essential process of testing your business ideas in the real world, gathering feedback, and confirming there's actual demand for your solution before going all-in. It's about resisting the temptation to fall blindly in love with your ideas and instead letting the market guide you to product-market fit. Prioritize getting your offer into the hands of real customers through pre-sales to see if the market truly wants what you have to offer.

Unlock exponential growth with the 80/20 Marketing Strategy. Automate and delegate your incremental marketing while doubling down on exponential plays. Harness the power of Dream 100 targeting, influencer marketing, strategic partnerships, and affiliate armies to scale fast.

Master the art of irresistible offers and authentic sales. Stack the value, minimize the risk, create urgency, and communicate your solution with clarity and conviction. Build trust with an enticing lead magnet, then guide your customers up the value ladder with a powerful core story and increasingly transformative offerings.

Bootstrap your way to success with creative funding strategies. Recruit an all-star team by leveraging talent platforms and forging win-win partnerships. Stay lean, agile, and resourceful, focusing on validating your MVP before overinvesting in infrastructure.

Transform your customers into raving fans and evangelists. Systematically maximize their lifetime value through strategic onboarding, ongoing nurturing, and relentless over-delivery. Create a community around your brand and make your business an irreplaceable part of your customers' lives and identities.

Achieve more by doing less with the 100X Ultimate Time Management Process. Ruthlessly focus on your vital few activities, constantly refine and improve your approach, and execute your plans with the discipline of unbreakable routines.

Lastly, continuously build your war chest of 100X Accelerators. Invest in your network, partnerships, personal brand, audience, automation, capital access, marketing systems, distribution channels, talent bench, and continuous learning. These are the force multipliers that will make everything else easier and create an unfair advantage in any market.

Above all, remember that this journey is as much about who you become as it is about what you achieve. Embrace the identity of the unstoppable entrepreneur, the relentless problem-solver, the bold value-creator. Fall in love with the process of constant and never-ending improvement and make the journey itself your ultimate reward.

As you embark on this path, know that you're not alone. You are part of a rising tide of entrepreneurs who are rewriting the rules of success and shaping the future of business. You're a trailblazer, a game-changer, a leader in the making.

So take a moment to appreciate how far you've come. Celebrate your courage in choosing this unconventional path and your commitment to mastering the art and science of entrepreneurship. You've equipped yourself with the mindsets, strategies, and tools to not just survive, but to thrive in the new economy.

But don't get complacent. The journey to $1 million is just the beginning. It's the launchpad for even greater impact, freedom, and fulfillment. With the foundations you've built and the momentum you've created, there's no limit to what you can achieve.

So dream bigger. Set your sights on $10 million, $100 million, and beyond. But more importantly, focus on the lives you'll touch, the problems you'll solve, and the legacy you'll leave. Because true success isn't just about the commas in your bank account—it's about the difference you make in the world.

You've got this. You're ready. The skills you've gained, the mindsets you've cultivated, the relationships you've built—these are your superpowers. Wield them with wisdom, integrity, and audacity.

So take a deep breath. Summon your courage. And take the first step on this incredible adventure.

A million-dollar future is yours for the taking. A life of impact, freedom, and joy is yours to create.

Let's make it happen, one bold move at a time.

I'll see you at the top.

RESOURCES

100X Entrepreneur's Club
If you want to be part of a community of like-minded individuals who are on their way to $1M in 12-18 months, then join our list of over 277,000 students.

Join the 100X Entrepreneur's Club for FREE today:
100xClub.ai

$0 to $1M Workbook
If you want the 130+ page PDF companion workbook for this Masterclass, you can purchase a copy here:
https://www.100xbusinessadvisor.com/workbook